"*Better Memory Now*" Series Presents:

VOCABULARY WORDS BRILLIANCE

Learn How to Quickly and Creatively Memorize Vocab!

By Luis Angel Echeverria
MEMORY MASTER CHAMPION &
Memory Coach with AE Mind at
www.AEMind.com

**Co-Author: Diana Ortiz,
University Student**

Copyright © 2017 by AE Mind. All Rights Reserved
The **images** used in the *How to Remember Names and Faces* book were **licensed** from ShutterStock.com.

No part of this publication may be reproduced, stored in retrieval system, or transmitted in any form or by any means, electronic, mechanical, photocopying, recording, without the direct consent of AE Mind and Luis Angel Echeverria.

YOUR GIFTS

As a bonus, you can get my latest **Free Better Memory Now Guide and Memory Training Videos** to help you with your ongoing continued memory improvement education!

Download Here:

www.AEMind.com/VocabBookGift

LEARN MORE / CONTACT

Learn more about Luis Angel's "Better Memory Now" programs and other Memory Training material for Professionals, Students, Memory Athletes, and Everyone Else, by going to:

www.AEMind.com

SOCIAL

YT: Youtube.com/aemind
FB: Facebook.com/aemind1
IG: ae.mind
Twitter: @aemind

Email: LuisAngel@AEMind.com

TESTIMONIALS

What others say about Luis Angel and The AE Mind: Better Memory Now System

Nathan Brais
Director of Student Life at Coastline College

"I just want to give a big shout out to Luis Angel Echeverria. Thank you so much for coming to our event. You're awesome, with a close to 500 students and staff here. You did 2 memory workshops for us, which the students were really impressed by, and I really appreciate you also doing our keynote address. **Luis is engaging and he's also great with students. He has a very energetic presence and I highly recommend him for any of your school events that you may be having for high school or for college group."**

DANNY BELTRAN
AE Mind Memory Athlete and Student at UC Irvine.

"Joining the AE Mind team has been one of the best decisions I've ever made. **I was taught to memorize so many things without having to tear my head apart and it is so useful in academics**, *not to mention* **everyday life.** *Luis is a great mentor and coach. Without him I wouldn't be in the position I'm in now. Thanks Luis for everything!"*

KASSANDRA CEJA
AE Mind Memory Athlete and Student at UC Irvine

"Meeting Luis and joining the AE Mind Team has been a great experience. Not only did we get the chance to compete in the memory competition in New York, but we also learned skills that helped us memorize material for our academic courses. **We also got the opportunity to learn strategies that would benefit us with our future careers**. Being on the team we learned lots of skills, it opened our doors to many new opportunities, we got to meet many inspiring people, and it was overall one of the best decisions I have made."

THANK YOU

**First and Foremost, GOD and Mom!
&
Everyone Who Helped Me along the way to achieving my goals!**

Special shout out to the contributing co-author, Diana Ortiz!

CONTENTS

ABOUT LUIS ANGEL ix
CONTRIBUTION x
FOREWORD xi

INTRO... 1
    Luis Angel's Journey as a Memory Coach........................... 5
    Visualize This 8
    Learning Vocabulary Words the AE Mind Way 10
    Legend Citation Key 17
    Getting Started Right... 18

UNIT 1 21
    Section 1
    Section 2

UNIT 2 31
    Section 3
    Section 4
    Section 5

UNIT 3 45
    Section 6
    Section 7
    Section 8
    Section 9

UNIT 4 63
    Section 10
    Section 11
    Section 12
    Section 13

UNIT 5 .... **81**
    Section 14
    Section 15
    Section 16
    Section 17
    Section 18

UNIT 6 .... **103**
    Section 19
    Section 20
    Section 21
    Section 22
    Section 23

UNIT 7 .... **125**
    Section 24
    Section 25
    Section 26
    Section 27
    Section 28

UNIT 8 .... **147**
    Section 29
    Section 30
    Section 31
    Section 32
    Section 33

Answers 169
Gift... 174
Contact 176

ABOUT LUIS ANGEL

- 1st Memory Master Champion on FOX's Superhuman

- **Founder** and Main Memory Coach at AE Mind | Accelerated Empowered Mind
- **Competed** in the USA Memory Championship

- **Was the Youngest American** to Compete in the World Memory Championship with TEAM USA
- **Memorized** a 120 Digit Number in 5 Minutes
- **Coached the AE Mind Memory Team** to a 1st Place Medal in the Numbers event at the USA Memory Championship
- **Started AE Mind Memory Clubs** in Los Angeles High Schools and in Universities such as UC Irvine and UC Santa Barbara.
- **Speaker** for Schools, Organizations, and Companies to help students and professionals have a "Better Memory Now"
- **Author and Creator of the AE Mind:** *Better Memory Now* **Series**

CONTRIBUTION

As someone who grew up in government-subsidized housing, on food stamps, and in an area with a lot of gang activity (never participated, but witnessed a lot of it around him), Luis Angel knows what it's like to have to go through struggle in life.

That's why Luis Angel loves contributing to help make the lives of those in need better in whichever way that he can.

GIVE BACK TUESDAY
Along with Living Waters and Countless of Amazing Volunteers, Luis Angel helps feed the homeless and families in need every Tuesday in the City of Santa Ana in Southern California.

FEED FAMILIES EVENT
Luis Angel has also partnered with Dion Jaffee, Bell High School, and several friends who donate to the cause to Feed Families every year for Thanksgiving!

A portion of the proceeds from the AE Mind Better Memory Now Live Events, Courses, and Books goes to continuing our Contribution Efforts!

Thank you in advance for your support!

FOREWORD

Luis Angel is one of the most genuine, superhuman (literally) I have met.

I had the privilege of meeting Angel at a give-back outreach, helping the homeless.
His heart for helping others is inevitable. He's always trying to find ways to help others and make a difference in the world. He uses his talent of memorization and recollection to help those of us who don't have as good of memory.

As seen on Fox, Luis Angel uses different tactics and cognition tools to help him remember difficult words and concepts. I have personally used some of his techniques to help study for my exams and also increase my ability to remember names. Let me tell you, it works!

This book will give you a glimpse of how Angel's mind works and how he forms connections between words and definitions. I hope this book will serve as a great introduction to the wonderful world of memory and I hope it will inspire you to start forming and creating associations for your next exam, project, memory competition or everyday use, so that you too can unlock the extraordinary power of memory.

Good luck!

-Diana Ortiz
UC Irvine Student, Co-Author of Vocabulary Words Brilliance

Intro

A juicy bone inside of an envelope is being torn open by a Siberian husky.

A very funny clown juggling golf balls in the air and they all fall on top of his head.

A grey car full of rice cranking up music as they dance, party, and socialize all while having a blast.

If you were able to see those stories clearly in your mind, then you are ready to learn how to memorize any vocabulary word with ease, just like all of the top memory athletes do it! I tell you what those stories represent in a moment, but first let me introduce myself and tell you how this book will help you out.

Hi, my name is Luis Angel, and I am your memory coach!

As someone who went from struggling in school to competing all over the world in memory competitions and eventually becoming the first Memory Master Champion on Superhuman, I am here to tell you that anyone can truly tap into their God Given Brilliant Gifts of Remembering Anything Quickly, by simply following a few simple steps that will be outlined in the book. The techniques that are distilled here will allow you to use your imagination to take vocabulary words and learn them in a very fun and creative manner. Just imagine what that would mean for you to be able to use such an amazing skill once perfected by continually practicing and making progress throughout the examples in this Vocabulary Words Brilliance Book. How will this help you in school, work, and just life in general. Because I promise you this, by mastering the ability of quickly memorizing any word and its meaning, you will also be able to apply this skill to any other area of education that wish to apply it to. I know that I'm making all of these promises and you might be thinking that this can't really work for everyone but only a selected few "smart" individuals, but let me reassure you that I myself was once in your shoes. I was seeking a way to just give me a little bit of an edge when it came to learning even the most basic of things.

Here's the thing, Bryan/Brenda (I like to give names to people that I haven't met yet. Actually, when I was in New York riding the subway, I was giving random names to people that were sitting

Introduction

near me and using the memory techniques that I'm going to teach you in this book to memorize their fake names. Sorry, this was a long side note. Let's continue...), memory is a fundamental part of our everyday existence. Whether it's in a very serious situation that can potentially lead to a distraught outcome, or a fun and playful setting where you cause your team to lose because you forgot a pattern that you needed to memorize, the act of forgetting can trigger one of the most painful emotions that a person can feel.

On the flip side of this, don't you feel a sense of euphoria when you are able to successfully recall something important. Maybe it was the correct answers to a test, or perhaps it was the name of that special person that you met the previous week. We love it when we are able to remember things that are near and dear to us and hate it when we struggle with our memory.

Throughout the last several years of me improving my own memory and helping individuals achieve their goals of being able to learn faster and remember better, I've come across this pattern of limiting beliefs that people have about themselves. Most individuals raise their hands when I ask the following question during my Better Memory Now Live Events, "Who here believes that they have either a terrible memory or would love it if they could better remember even just day to day tasks?" From students to business professionals, people from all ages want to learn the secret formula on how to improve their memory and they want it NOW!

Well if you are one of those individuals who fits into that category then you're in luck because I'm about to release the magic sauce, RIGHT NOW!

The Key to Memorization is... VISUALIZATION!

That's it.
Simple.
Easy.
Done.

There is a catch. You see I compete all over the world in memory competitions and every one of my memory athlete friends will tell you that what they do to memorize a large amount of information in a short period of time, is that they visualize and create quirky stories in order to remember that info. To be one of the best memorizers however, the requirements are that you need to practice consistently. You don't take an easy fix pill or someone waves a magic wand over your head and all of a sudden, you're reciting the first 1000 digits of pi. You need to put in some effort into taking this simple to learn concept and being able to use it to remember, say your grocery list.

My response to the question of "can ANYONE learn how to do this?" is always that as long as the person doesn't have any serious physical brain disabilities or disorders, then of course the answer is "YES!" Certain individuals have had serious brain trauma that impairs them from fully being able to embrace the techniques taught here, but the majority of the people that approach this with an open mind can definitely use the memory techniques to memorize and learn any information at an accelerated rate. I've worked with people that have ADHD, focus problems, dyslexia, early onset signs of dementia, and even individuals that are blind, and every one of them have had success with being able to improve their memory skills. I myself was diagnosed with Attention Deficit Disorder and have been able to turn that situation around after being introduced to this world of competitive memorization.

Introduction

THE LUIS ANGEL STORY

When I raised the trophy as the first memory master champion on the first episode of Superhuman, I couldn't hold back the tears that soon were flowing out of my eyes and going down my cheeks as I thought back to all the struggles that I had up to that point. Just a few years prior to this moment, my grades were suffering greatly in school, I almost getting fired from my job, and was not a good place with my everyday life. Everything around me was going in a downward spiral in which I felt like I had no control over.

At school, I had a 1.0 GPA my freshman year, and graduated by having a 1.75 GPA my senior year in high school. I had to repeat several classes in between those years because my brain was just not retaining the information that it needed to. I couldn't focus, I couldn't concentrate, and I couldn't remember all that well. When I finally did graduate, I thought that things were going to be different in college. That wasn't the case, because I ended up getting kicked out of school for my continued efforts of not doing great in my classes.

I was on the verge of getting fired from my job at a satellite TV company because of my forgetfulness. I would constantly lose my tools and would fail to remember the procedures of installing the satellite dishes on people's homes. There were plenty of times when the following happened. I would be up on a roof to get ready to drill the dish onto the black tar that I had just placed on top of the shingles, when I would realize that I was missing a bolt. I would go down the ladder while carrying my heavy tool belt and go straight to the van. Along the way, something must have happened to my train of thought because as soon as I opened the van's door I would wonder what I was supposed to get. I would go back up to the top of the house to see if I could get a trigger to remind me and then it would hit me. "I need a bolt, I need a bolt, I need a bolt…" I kept repeating to myself over and over again. This instance and several others were making me cost the company a lot of money and they had already given me tons of warnings to improve my ability to perform the tasks at hand or face the ultimate consequence of getting the pink slip.

At home, things such as remembering whether I ate or not became a fixture for my everyday life. My mom would ask me at 3 PM on a Saturday after she got home from work, "mijo ya comiste/son did you eat?" I couldn't give her an answer because I honestly didn't remember. Another one of my favorites was walking into my room knowing that I was there to get something of importance and staring at the bed for a good 60 seconds only to realize that I had forgotten why I was in that room in the first place. Events like these were constant recurrences that I knew had to be stopped or at least dramatically tamed back several notches.

The last straw happened on an island off the coast of Southern California called, Catalina Island. I was there to install cable. When we go out to the island, we need to place all of the tools and equipment that we are going to need for each one of the jobs inside of a large plastic bin. We then board the ferry and travel afloat the pacific waters for 45 minutes. Well dummy me ended up leaving behind several tools and satellite dish parts that were required to complete each job. I remember sitting on a bench waiting the three hours until my ferry came to pick me up. I had just cancelled all of the jobs that I had for the day and was thinking to myself that I was getting fired. As I saw out onto the crashing waves, I felt like my world was also crashing down on me.
My mind just kept reviewing all of the negative situations that had led me to this point. All of those times that I kept forgetting. All of those times that I couldn't remember something. Every single time that I lacked focus at school, work, and in my personal life. I was seeing all of the pain that this had cost me and how painful my life was going to be if I continue to remain stuck in the same pattern. I began to shed tears upon tears. My vision was blurry. I cried. I sobbed. I had pity. I had regret. I was a total mess.

"God help me find a solution to this misery!" I yelled out in my mind hoping that he would hear.

And then, it hit me. He answered my prayers because I instantly knew what I had to do.

There was a gentleman a few years back that did a seminar where he memorized the names of hundreds of people in the audience and repeated all of them from memory. He then taught

Introduction

everyone in attendance how to do what he had just done. I wasn't there, but my friend Dion was.

"D, I need to know that memory guy's name. Do you remember it?"

He told me, "yea it's Ron White."

As soon as I got home, I went online and got the memory course and went through it immediately. I quickly put the memory techniques to use and saw results right away. I was able to memorize a list of words in a matter of minutes. I memorized a long number and repeated it forward and backwards. I was able to remember the names of the people that I had met. More importantly, it helped me in every area of life that I was previously struggling with because of my memory problems. At school, I went from getting kicked out for a semester to getting straight A's. I went from almost getting fired from my job to getting a promotion and becoming the youngest technician to hold that new position at my office. I went from forgetting the basics at home, to competing all over the world in memory competitions. This is what led me to compete in the Superhuman show and become the 1st Memory Master Champion!

I have also trained other students who have gone on to compete in memory competitions and they have taken home Gold in national events. All of my students that have graduated from high school are now attending high ranking universities here in California. One of the schools that I work with, Bell High School, was featured with me on the show Superhuman. I am much prouder of what they have achieved than what I did, because it shows that with a little bit of hard work anyone can learn how to use these memory techniques in every area of life!

Visualize This

You're walking up to a young lady with curly hair at a party and you two exchange names. She tells you that her name is Paris S. and that she is from Chicago Illinois. You instantly picture the Eiffel Tower with snakes wrapped around it trying to reach a deep-dish Chicago style pizza at the top of her Paris' curly hair.

Why are you seeing all of this?

Because you have learned that the Key to Memorization is Visualization and that the best way to remember something important, is to create a quirky visual story. All of the top memory athletes from around the world use this same technique in international memory championships. I've competed alongside them in several of the competitions. One in particular made me the first Memory Master Champion on the hit TV show, Superhuman!

I was sitting on the chair with my hands covering my face as I prayed for a calm and clear mind because I knew that millions of people were going to be watching from home. When my hands came down, the image flashed on the large screen. A young lady with curly hair who I had seen earlier that day. She was one of over 100 audience members which I had to memorize the personal information of, prior to me heading out and taking center stage. I had to memorize their first name, last name initial, hometown (city, state), and a feature about them. As I looked at her face on the screen, my brain immediately scanned through the hundreds of stories that I created to help me remember the 500+ pieces of information. There were a few ladies in the audience with curly hair, but this one was unique. As I waved my hands around in the air to help me get a clearer picture and narrow down her name and hometown, it hit me!
"Paris S. from Chicago, Illinois," I told the Superhuman host, Kal Penn.

"Are you sure?" he says.

"Sure he's sure," yells out Mike Tyson. "That's why he's in that chair!"

Introduction

I smiled and told Kal to lock in that answer.

As she stood up from out in the audience, she says, "my name is Paris S. and I'm from Chicago, Illinois."

I jumped up with sheer excitement and joy! And as I continued to get every single one of these correctly, I became very grateful that these memory techniques came into my life. I hugged my mom, my entire family, my friend's Dion and Feibi, the host, the panelist, all of the contestants, and of course my mentor Ron White.

He was on the show with me and also nailed his challenge of quickly memorizing a ton of numbers, names, faces, and facts about the people that he met. I got real emotional as I thanked him for everything that he had done for me and for teaching this kid from the LA County city of La Puente, how to use his full mind's power to achieve what seemed impossible a few years earlier. In order to get over my struggles in school and in life, he taught me that I needed to just let my creativity flow through as I reviewed the information that I wanted to remember.

I am here to be that guiding hand for you as you embark on this journey of unlocking the true power of your mind's ability to hold onto information. Just as the gift was given to me by my mentor, I am going to share that gift with you. Realize that if you were able to remember that Eiffel Tower with snakes and a deep-dish Chicago pizza, then you too can become a memory master!

Learning Vocabulary Words the AE Mind Way

Let's say that you needed to learn the following words:

Benevolent = Well Meaning and Kindly
Tawdry = Showy but cheap and of poor quality
Languid = Weak or Slow and Relaxed
Gregarious = Fond of company; sociable
Pulchritude = Beauty
Tumult = Disorder; loud confused noise by a mass of people
Perusal = The action of reading or examining something
Redolent = Fragrant or sweet-smelling
Guffaw = A loud laugh
Abasement = humiliation or degradation

In order to learn them in an accelerated manner like the top memory athletes do, what you want to do is create a picture for the word and then link that to the definition by creating a story out of it. Just do a direct link between the word and the definition, then make sure to review them over time.

Here are the stories that I created for each word:

Benevolent = I gave my dog a **Bone** inside of an **Envelope** because he was *being kind* all week.

Tawdry = A **Towel** couldn't **Dry** the wet floor because it was made of *cheap material*.

Languid = On top of a **Lane** there was a **Squid** laying there very *weak and lazy* like.

Gregarious = Inside of the **Gray Car**, there was a lot of **Rice** *having fun and talking with each other*.

Pulchritude = The **Poker cards** that the **Toad** had were a straight flush which caused a *beautiful* princess to appear.

Tumult = A **Tooth Mowing** his neighbor's lawn which causes the neighbor to get *upset and yell* at the tooth.

Perusal = **Parrot** poured **Salt** on the book he was *reading*.

Redolent = I used a **Red Deodorant** to cover up the *smell* coming from my armpits.

Guffaw = The clown threw **Golf balls** up in there and they landed on top of his head which made him *laugh out loud*.

Abasement = The guy was shoved into the **Basement** and was completely *humiliated*.

Introduction

Vocabulary Quiz

Match the Words with its proper definition.

1. Abasement _____
2. Benevolent _____
3. Gregarious _____
4. Guffaw _____
5. Languid _____

6. Perusal _____
7. Pulchritude _____
8. Redolent _____
9. Tawdry _____
10. Tumult _____

a. Fragrant or sweet-smelling
b. Disorder; loud confused noise
c. The action of reading
d. Showy but cheap and of poor quality
e. Fond of company; sociable

f. Beauty
g. A loud laugh
h. Weak or Slow and Relaxed
i. Humiliation or degradation
j. Well Meaning and Kindly

Introduction

Answers for Vocab Quiz

1. i
2. j
3. e
4. g
5. h

6. c
7. f
8. a
9. d
10. b

How did you do with that vocab quiz? Did you get them all correct? Notice how you were able to think of the visual triggers as you were matching the words with the definitions.

Throughout this book, you will see 165 more words, definitions, and the stories that myself and my co-author, Diana, came up with to help you memorize those words. Some of the stories and associations may or may not resonate with you and by all means feel free to go ahead and create your own stories to help you remember them.

Once you go through all of these words, freely apply this method to any other vocabulary that you need to commit to memory. Whether it's in your English class or Science classes, you can use this creative story telling technique to memorize a vast amount of information in a short period of time. Just make sure to review them in a spaced period of time in order to move the information from short term memory to long term memory.

Bonus

If a word has an letter in it that I need help with remembering it, I usually throw in my picture for the single letters. For example, if the word was "Blithe," I'll picture a bat biting with leaves on it. The leaves would give me an extra trigger to help me remember the "L" in "Blithe."

Here are the Alphabet Pictures

A = APPLE
B = BALL
C = CAT
D = DOG
E = ELEPHANT
F = FROG
G = GOLFBALL
H = HAND
I = IGLOO
J = JACK
K = KANGAROO
L = LEAF
M = MAT

N = NAIL
O = ORANGE
P = PICKLE
Q = QUEEN (CROWN)
R = RHINO
S = SNAKE
T = TOWEL
U = UMBRELLA
V = VIOLIN
W = WATER
X = XYLOPHONE
Y = YOYO
Z = ZEBRA

Introduction

Legend Key Citations

Throughout the vocabulary words sections you will see the keys below which indicates where the reference citations are from for each word and definition.

[g] = Google.com

[d] = Dictionary.com

[t] = Thesaurus.com

[m] = Merriam-Webster.com

[a] = American Heritage® Dictionary of the English Language, Fifth Edition. (2011)

[c] = Collins English Dictionary – Complete and Unabridged, 12th Edition 2014 © HarperCollins Publishers 2014

Getting Started Right

Remember that this entire process is going to be a partnership.

I have gone to many seminars and read many books where the speaker or author does a one-way interaction with the audience and expects them to be experts in that topic when they're done.

That's not how accelerated learning works.

At every single one of my seminars or events, whether I'm teaching a group of thousands of people or just doing a one-on-one training, the way that I teach is very interactive. I teach you how to be a creative story teller in order to memorize information through my own examples, and then you go ahead and create your own stories to help you memorize new material.

So, get ready to stretch your mind. Be like a parachute and allow your mind to work by being open to the ideas presented in this book. They have been tested all over the world by the best memorizers and they simply work when I applied correctly.

Introduction

HONEST REVIEW

I love seeing the transformation that people go through when they learn this system, and I would be extremely grateful if you helped contribute to that transformation.

When you get a chance, if you could take about a minute or two to go to the Vocabulary Words Brilliance Book Page and leave a Review, you will truly be helping to improve the lives of thousands of people who struggle with their memory.

Thank You in Advance!
Other than that, let the show begin!

Enjoy, and Much Success on your journey to have an AE Mind!

(Copyright/Legal Info Because all of the images used in this book are licensed images, meaning we purchased the rights to use the images in this book, we must let you know that the images used in this book cannot be reproduced, stored in a retrieval system, or transmitted in any form or by any means, electronic, mechanical, photocopying, recording, without our direct consent. If you would like to get the licenses to use these images, please go to: www.ShutterStock.com.)

Thank you for understanding.

UNIT 1

SECTION 1

Advocate (v): A person who publicly supports or recommends a particular cause or policy. [g]

Synonyms [t]: *backer, defender, promoter*
Antonyms [t]: *opponent, assailant, protestor*

Word Use
He advocated higher salaries for teachers.

Pictures
advocate = avocado
Definition = speaking into microphone

Story = The avocado was speaking into a microphone as it was praising the carrot that was running for congress.

Conciliate (v): stop (someone) from being angry or discontented; placate; pacify. [g]

Synonyms *[t]: calm, irenic, quiet*
Antonyms *[t]: fighting, refusing, stubborn*

<u>Word Use</u> [d]
to conciliate an angry competitor.

<u>Pictures</u>
Conciliate = Cone + latte
Definition = give someone who is mad

Story = The kid gave his mom a cone with latte flavored ice cream to help her calm down from yelling at him all day for ruining her new dress.

--------------- --------------- --------------- --------------- ---------------

Eclectic (adj): deriving ideas, style, or taste from a broad and diverse range of sources. [g]

Synonyms *[t]: broad, varied, assorted*
Antonyms *[t]: like, narrow, particular*

<u>Word Use</u> [d]
Forty-eight works from 37 artists, including 18 women, are on display, and the selection is eclectic.

<u>Pictures</u>
Eclectic = Electric (guitar)
Definition = Vast variety/style

Story = The man playing the electric guitar was playing a vast variety of genres.

Exonerated (v): To free from blame. [a]

Synonyms *[t]: acquit, free*
Antonyms *[t]: blame, convict, damn*

Word Use [d]
He was exonerated from the accusation of cheating.

Pictures
Exonerated = Egg salad + rat
Definition = eaten by someone else

Story = The egg salad was eaten by the rat and not the monkey, so the monkey was found innocent and set free from prison.

--------------   --------------   --------------   --------------   --------------

Inane (adj): Lacking sense or substance. [a]

Synonyms *[t]: urd, daft, flat*
Antonyms *[t]: bright, intelligent, smart*

Word Use [d]
Sheen denies everything, calling the claims " laughable and inane."

Pictures
Inane = In and Out
Definition = Out of hamburgers

Story = In and out was out of hamburgers and it made no sense.

Section 1 Quiz

1. Advocate __
2. Conciliate __
3. Eclectic __
4. Exonerated __
5. Inane __

a. Deriving ideas, style, or taste from a broad and diverse range of sources.
b. A person who publicly supports or recommends a particular cause or policy.
c. Stop (someone) from being angry or discontented
d. To free from blame.
e. Lacking sense or substance.

Check your answers in the back of the book.

SECTION 2

Acumen (n): The ability to make good judgments and quick decisions, typically in a particular domain. [g]

Synonyms [t]: *awareness, brilliance, wit*
Antonyms [t]: *ignorance, mistake, inability*

Word Use [d]
Remarkable acumen in business matters.

Pictures
acumen = Acute angle + men
Definition = running fast towards brain

Story = The acute angle shot the men running fast towards the brain.

Filial (adj): Of, relating to, or befitting a son or daughter: filial respect. [a]

Synonyms [t]: *daughterly, familial, sororal*
Antonyms [t]: *n/a*

Word Use [d]
She explained that "filial laws" are a vestige of English rule.

Pictures
Filial = File + nail
Definition = affectionate

Story = The father took her daughter to the nail salon to get her nails file down to show his affectionate for her.

--------------- --------------- --------------- --------------- ---------------

Laud (v): To give praise to; glorify. [a]

Synonyms [t]: *admire, adore, extol*
Antonyms [t]: *abhor, blame, hate*

Word Use [d]
Israel is quick to laud those who fought the Nazis, no matter how futilely, over those who went powerless to their deaths.

Pictures
Laud = Lord
Definition = Praising God

Story = Everyone at church was giving praise to our lord and savior, Jesus Christ.

Nonchalant (adj): Casually unconcerned or indifferent. [a]

Synonyms [t]: *aloof, casual, calm*
Antonyms [t]: *biased, careful, hard*

Word Use [d]
His nonchalant manner infuriated me.

Pictures
Nonchalant = Nun + challenge
Definition = calm and unconcerned

Story = The nun at the church was calm and unconcerned with the bible challenge because she had been preparing months prior.

--------------   --------------   --------------   --------------   --------------

Perquisites (n): a thing regarded as a special right or privilege enjoyed as a result of one's position. [g]

Synonyms [t]: *perk, extra, tip*
Antonyms [t]: *disadvantage, loss*

Word Use [d]
Among the president's perquisites were free use of a company car and paid membership in a country club.

Pictures
Perquisites = Pear + Cuisine
Definition = Benefits

Story = The pear was the most popular fruit in the cuisine because it had so many health benefits.

Section 2 Quiz

1. Acumen ___
2. Filial ___
3. Laud ___
4. Perquisites ___
5. Nonchalant ___

a. A thing regarded as a special right or privilege enjoyed as a result of one's position.
b. Of, relating to, or befitting a son or daughter.
c. To give praise to; glorify.
d. Casually unconcerned or indifferent.
e. The ability to make good judgments and quick decisions, typically in a particular domain.

Remember to check your answers in the back of the book when you are done with each quiz.

UNIT 2

SECTION 3

Anachronism (n): The representation of someone as existing or something as happening in other than chronological, proper, or historical order. [a]

Synonyms *[t]: misplacement, prolepsis, solecism*
Antonyms *[t]: orderly*

Word Use [d]
The sword is an anachronism in modern warfare.

Pictures
Anachronism = Ants + Chrome watch
Definition = "moving without order"

Story = The ants were running around chaotically inside the chrome watch.

Coalition (n): An alliance, especially a temporary one, of people, factions, parties, or nations. [a]

***Synonyms** [t]: bloc, fusion, ring*
***Antonyms** [t]: disunion, division, divorce*

Word Use [d]
Not everyone signed up for the coalition, she says, noting that the Komen foundation did not join.

Pictures
Coalition = Coal + Lit
Definition = Coal burning and vanishing

Story = The coal was so lit with flames that it only lasted temporary and quickly vanished.

--------------- --------------- --------------- --------------- ---------------

Dearth (n): A scarce supply; a lack. [a]

***Synonyms** [t]: ence, shortage, lack*
***Antonyms** [t]: abundance, plenty, wealth*

Word Use [d]
There is a dearth of good engineers.

Pictures
Dearth = Dark + Earth
Definition = Lack of sunlight

Story = It became a dark earth because there was a lack of sunlight.

Endorsed (v): Declare one's public approval or support of. [g]

Synonyms [t]: *approved, supported, sealed*
Antonyms [t]: *disapproved, cancelled, vetoed*

Word Use [d]
To endorse a political candidate.

Pictures
Endorsed = In doors
Definition = stamp of approval

Story = The carpenter signed the door with his name and gave it the stamp of approval to say that it was certified and fully inspected.

--------------- --------------- --------------- --------------- ---------------

Gratuitous (adj): Given or granted without return or recompense; unearned. [a]

Synonyms [t]: *chargeless, gratis, willing*
Antonyms [t]: *costly, expensive, warranted*

Word Use [d]
A gratuitous insult.

Pictures
Gratuitous = Crate + Tut (king)
Definition = Placed in crate

Story = The slaves opened the crate and placed King Tut in there for no reason.

Section 3 Quiz

1. Anachronism ___
2. Coalition ___
3. Dearth ___
4. Endorsed ___
5. Gratuitous ___

a. Given or granted without return or recompense; unearned.
b. Declare one's public approval or support of.
c. An alliance, especially a temporary one, of people, factions, parties, or nations.
d. The representation of someone as existing or something as happening in other than chronological, proper, or historical order.
e. A scarce supply; a lack.

SECTION 4

Bigamy (n): the act of going through a marriage ceremony while already married to another person. [a]

Synonyms [t]: n/a
Antonyms [t]: n/a

Word Use [d]
Some are demanding a national marriage law, that a man legally married in one State may not be a bigamist in another.

Pictures
Bigamy = Big Army Officer
Definition = Married two ladies

Story = The big Army Officer married one woman in France and another in Germany.

Jocular (adj): Characterized by joking. [a]

Synonyms [t]: *cheerful, jolly, boffo*
Antonyms [t]: *depressed, sad, unhappy*

Word Use [d]
Jocular remarks about opera stars.

Pictures
Jocular = Jock + muscular
Definition = Jokes

Story = The jock was making jokes with his friends by saying he was the most muscular teen in the school.

---------------   ---------------   ---------------   ---------------   ---------------

Landlord (n): One that owns and rents land, buildings, or dwelling units. [a]

Synonyms [t]: *freeholder, hotelier, saw*
Antonyms [t]: *boarder, leaser, renter*

Word Use [d]
But when our building was granted landmark status, our landlord tripled the rents.

Pictures
Landlord = Land + Lard
Definition = own land

Story = The farmer owned acres of land where he kept his pigs, later to be used as lard.

Pennant (n): a flag denoting a sports championship or other achievement. [g]

Synonyms *[t]: streamer, color, jack*
Antonyms *[t]: n/a*

Word Use [d]
In the midst of this, almost unnoticed, the Yankees clinched the pennant.

Pictures
Pennant = Pen + Tent
Definition = Flag

Story = At a basketball summer camp the winning team grabbed their flag and a pen in order to tag their basketball's team name on it. Afterwards they placed it on their tent for all to see.

--------------- --------------- --------------- --------------- ---------------

Ravage (v): To bring heavy destruction on; devastate [a]

Synonyms *[t]: consume, damage, demolish*
Antonyms *[t]: aid, assist, create*

Word Use [d]
It also can ravage entire public health systems meant to bring children safely into the world.

Pictures
Ravage = Roof + sewage
Definition = Hit by a tornado

Story = The roof was full of sewage and it deteriorated when the tornado hit.

Unit 2

Section 4 Quiz

1. Bigamy ___
2. Jocular ___
3. Landlord ___
4. Pennant ___
5. Ravage ___

a. the act of going through a marriage ceremony while already married to another person.
b. One that owns and rents land, buildings, or dwelling units.
c. Characterized by joking.
d. To bring heavy destruction on; devastate
e. a flag denoting a sports championship or other achievement.

SECTION 5

Arcane (adj): Known or understood by only a few. [a]

Synonyms [t]: *esoteric, mystic, occult*
Antonyms [t]: *common, known, normal*

Word Use [d]
She knew a lot about Sanskrit grammar and other arcane matters.

Pictures
Arcane = Arcade
Definition = "Known by few"

Story = Out of all the kids that tried, only one smart kid knew how to beat the guitar hero game in the arcade.

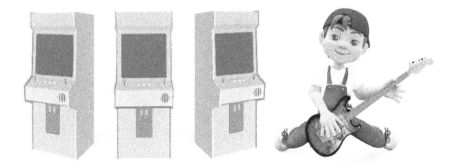

Dichotomies (n): A division into two contrasting things or parts. [a]

Synonyms [t]: *difference of, opinion, disagreement*
Antonyms [t]: *likeness, similarity, agreement*

Word Use [d]
A dichotomy between thought and action.

Pictures
Dichotomies = Die + economy
Definition = two different things

Story = When a flower dies it has no effect on the economy because they're two different things.

--------------- --------------- --------------- --------------- ---------------

Forejudge (v): To judge beforehand without adequate examination or evidence; prejudge. [a]

Synonyms [t]: *decide, presume*
Antonyms [t]: *n/a*

Word Use [d]
"We will go to America before you forejudge it altogether," said he.

Pictures
Forejudge = Forehead + judge
Definition = Guilty (slamming gavel)

Story = The prisoner with a tattoo on his forehead pleaded to the judge his innocence but the judge without adequate evidence, slammed the gavel and found him guilty.

Usurp (v): To seize and hold (the power or rights of another, for example) by force or without legal authority. [a]

Synonyms *[t]: annex, grab, take*
Antonyms *[t]: give, keep, offer*

Word Use [d]
The pretender tried to usurp the throne.

Pictures
Usurp = Surf
Definition = Took my friends surfboard without consent.

Story = The waiter took my friends surf-board without consent and would not give it back so we had to call the police.

--------------- --------------- --------------- --------------- ---------------

Zephyr (n): Something that is airy, insubstantial, or passing. [a]

Synonyms *[t]: draft, puff, sky*
Antonyms *[t]: n/a*

Word Use
The zephyr was very calming and cooling in the summer heat.

Pictures
Zephyr = Zephyrus
Definition = wind

Story = In Greek mythology, Zephyrus was the god of the west wind.

Section 5 Quiz

1. Arcane ___
2. Dichotomies ___
3. Forejudge ___
4. Usurp ___
5. Zephyr ___

a. A division into two contrasting things or parts.
b. To seize and hold (the power or rights of another, for example) by force or without legal authority.
c. To judge beforehand without adequate examination or evidence; prejudge.
d. Something that is airy, insubstantial, or passing.
e. Known or understood by only a few.

As a reminder, please feel free to leave a review on the Vocabulary Words Brilliance Book Page where you purchased this book to help us get this in the hands of more individuals who want to improve their abilities of being able to remember their vocab! Thank you in advance!

UNIT 3

SECTION 6

Disillusioned (n): disappointed in someone or something that one discovers to be less good than one had believed. [g]

Synonyms [t]: disenchanted, embittered, broken
Antonyms [t]: enchanted, encouraged, enthusiastic

Word Use [d]
Phoenix fully inhabits Freddie Quell, a disillusioned paint thinner-guzzling WWII Navy veteran prone to fits of rage.

Pictures
Disillusioned = Disc + illusion
Definition = Wrong

Story = The songs on the disc gave a wrong illusion to the audience, the audience were not pleased and became ill.

Unit 3

Effusive (adj): Unrestrained or excessive in emotional expression; gushy. [a]

Synonyms [t]: lavish, gabby, windy
Antonyms [t]: apathetic, quiet, silent

Word Use [d]
Entertainment blog Holy Moly is among the most effusive with praise.

Pictures
Effusive = A Fuse
Definition = A lot of energy

Story = The tiny fuse contained so much energy that it was gushing everywhere.

--------------- --------------- --------------- --------------- ---------------

Fulcrum (n): The point or support on which a lever pivots. [a]

Synonyms [t]: clue, code, core
Antonyms [t]: exterior, outside, lock

Word Use [d]
It is, for these two sons, both born in 1964, the fulcrum for their great labors.

Pictures
Fulcrum = Falcon + Rim
Definition = standing at the top point.

Story = The falcon was resting at the very top of the car rim to support itself.

Insolence (adj): Audaciously rude or disrespectful; impertinent or impudent. [a]

***Synonyms** [t]: abuse, audacity, gall*
***Antonyms** [t]: approval, caution, respect*

Word Use [d]
But it seemed to him she had behaved with a pride that bordered on insolence.

Pictures
Insolence = In Sol (sun) dancing
Definition = dancing chaotically

Story = The sun was dancing chaotically all over the dance floor at the party and burned everyone he came across.

--------------   --------------   --------------   --------------   --------------

Quiescent (adj): In a state or period of inactivity or dormancy. [g]

***Synonyms** [t]: asleep, fallow, idle*
***Antonyms** [t]: active*

Word Use [d]
A quiescent mind.

Pictures
Quiescent = Quiet + scene
Definition = asleep

Story = During the filming of the movie, the actors had to act as if they were asleep to avoid the mummies from capturing them. it was a quiet and suspenseful scene.

Section 6 Quiz

1. Disillusioned ___
2. Effusive ___
3. Fulcrum ___
4. Insolence ___
5. Quiescent ___

a. In a state or period of inactivity or dormancy.
b. disappointed in someone or something that one discovers to be less good than one had believed.
c. The point or support on which a lever pivots.
d. Audaciously rude or disrespectful; impertinent or impudent.
e. Unrestrained or excessive in emotional expression; gushy.

SECTION 7

Analogy (n): A similarity in some respects between things that are otherwise dissimilar. [a]

Synonyms [t]: *comparison, correlation, parallel*
Antonyms [t]: *difference, dissimilarity, unlikeness*

Word Use [d]
I see no analogy between your problem and mine.

Pictures
Analogy = Ants + Log
Definition= "Comparing two different things"

Story = The ants were comparing the similarities between the ridges on the log to the veins on the leaf.

Bucolic (adj): Of or characteristic of the countryside or its people; rustic. [a]

Synonyms [t]: *agrarian, country, agricultural*
Antonyms [t]: *n/a*

Word Use [d]
They are both in the study of my old farmhouse, in a room that has three nice sized windows, each with a lovely, bucolic view.

Pictures
Bucolic = Broccoli
Definition = Binoculars (view) + farmhouse

Story = The farmer used his binoculars to watch the broccoli grow by his farmhouse.

--------------   --------------   --------------   --------------   --------------

Perusal (v): To read or examine, typically with great care. [a]

Synonyms [t]: *examination, inspection, research*
Antonyms [t]: *ignorance, neglect*

Word Use [d]
A more careful perusal yields this conclusion.

Pictures
Perusal = Peru (country) + Soul
Definition = Examine

Story = Peru has just pass a new law enforcing to examine the souls of every incoming soldier to make sure they are trustworthy.

Rectitude (n): The quality or condition of being correct in judgment. [a]

Synonyms [t]: *decency, honesty, integrity*
Antonyms [t]: *deceit, corruption, dishonesty*

Word Use [d]
Maybe it is his own reputation for rectitude, a reputation buttressed by the lack of scandals in his administration.

Pictures
Rectitude = Rock + Attitude
Definition = correct judgment

Story = Two geologist were competing to see how many rocks they could identify and make correct judgment of how old they were, after many hours of competing the both competitors had great attitudes.

--------------- --------------- --------------- --------------- ---------------

Usury (n): The practice of lending money and charging the borrower interest, especially at an exorbitant or illegally high rate. [a]

Synonyms [t]: *exploitation, stealing*
Antonyms [t]: *n/a*

Word Use [d]
On January 29, Francis referred to usury as "a dramatic social ill."

Pictures
Usury = Shore
Definition = High interest rate

Story = Sally by the sea-shore was selling her seashells when the owner of the property came to charge her rent with a very high interest rate.

Section 7 Quiz

1. Analogy ___
2. Bucolic ___
3. Perusal ___
4. Rectitude ___
5. Usury ___

a. The quality or condition of being correct in judgment.
b. The practice of lending money and charging the borrower interest, especially at an exorbitant or illegally high rate.
c. A similarity in some respects between things that are otherwise dissimilar.
d. To read or examine, typically with great care.
e. Of or characteristic of the countryside or its people; rustic.

SECTION 8

Capricious (adj): Characterized by, arising from, or subject to caprice; impulsive or unpredictable. [a]

Synonyms [t]: arbitrary, cold, odd
Antonyms [t]: cautious, stable, staid

Word Use [d]
He's such a capricious boss I never know how he'll react.

Pictures
Capricious – Capri sun juice pouch
Definition = not knowing if there is juice in the pouch

Story = Sometimes there's no juice in the Capri sun pouch, and other times there's an abundance of juice.

Fabrication (v): To make; create. [a]

***Synonyms** [t]: deceit, fake, jazz*
***Antonyms** [t]: truth, fun, reality*

Word Use [d]
His account of the robbery is a complete fabrication.

Pictures
Fabrication = Fabric cloth
Definition = stitched together

Story = The mother stitched together a fabric cloth to create a soft blanket.

--------------- --------------- --------------- --------------- ---------------

Inscribe (v): To write, print, carve, or engrave (words or letters) on or in a surface. [a]

***Synonyms** [t]: carve, etch, list*
***Antonyms** [t]: forget*

Word Use [d]
To inscribe a circle in a square.

Pictures
Inscribe = Insect + Scribble
Definition = write

Story = The flying insect was trying to stay still while he tried writing but the wind made it impossible and all he could do was scribbles.

Ordeal (n): A difficult or painful experience, especially one that severely tests character or endurance. [a]

Synonyms [t]: agony, trial, cross
Antonyms [t]: comfort, joy, peace

Word Use [d]
Every visit to a hospital is an ordeal but for those who cannot pay for private care the experience is a horror show.

Pictures
Ordeal = Oar + deal
Definition = fast river current

Story = As we kayaked down the river, we used the oar to deal with the quick and chaotic current moving ahead.

--------------   --------------   --------------   --------------   --------------

Preponderate (v): To exceed something else in weight. [a]

Synonyms [t]: boss, direct, sway
Antonyms [t]: follow, lose, serve

Word Use [d]
Evidence for the accused preponderated at the trial.

Pictures
Preponderate = meal prep + pond + deer
Definition = Heavy deer.

Story = The food in the meal prep container was so good that the deer couldn't resist eating it. The deer became so heavy when it went to the pond to float it nearly sank.

Unit 3

Section 8 Quiz

1. Capricious ___
2. Fabrication ___
3. Inscribe ___
4. Ordeal ___
5. Preponderate ___

a. A difficult or painful experience, especially one that severely tests character or endurance.
b. To exceed something else in weight.
c. Characterized by, arising from, or subject to caprice; impulsive or unpredictable.
d. To write, print, carve, or engrave (words or letters) on or in a surface.
e. To make; create.

SECTION 9

Decimate (v): kill, destroy, or remove a large percentage or part of. [g]

Synonyms [t]: *annihilation, cataclysm, devastation*
Antonyms [t]: *miracle, wonder, good fortune*

Word Use [d]
The population was decimated by a plague.

Pictures
Decimate = Dice + Might (strong)
Definition = destroy the town

Story = The huge dice used he's strong might to roll on the town and destroy the buildings.

Endurance (n): The ability or strength to continue or last, especially despite fatigue, stress, or other adverse conditions; stamina. [a]

Synonyms [t]: ability, vitality, moxie
Antonyms [t]: apathy, lack, fear

Word Use [d]
He has amazing physical endurance.

Pictures
Endurance = Dorito + Ranch
Definition = Plenty of ranch dip

Story = I love dipping my Doritos into ranch because the ranch never seems to run out.

--------------- --------------- --------------- --------------- ---------------

Instill (v): To introduce by gradual, persistent efforts; implant. [a]

Synonyms [t]: diffuse, imbue, infix
Antonyms [t]: takeout, neglect, halt

Word Use [d]
To instill courtesy in a child.

Pictures
Instill = in+steel
Definition = implant

Story = The dentist was ready to put an implant in the patient's mouth but noticed that the material used was steel instead of titanium.

Nocturnal (adj): Of, relating to, or occurring in the night. [a]

Synonyms [t]: *nightly, nighttime, late*
Antonyms [t]: *daytime*

Word Use [d]
Nocturnal visit.

Pictures
Nocturnal = Knock + Turn
Definition = night

Story = One late night the Uber driver knocked the stop sign down when he turned the wrong direction.

--------------   --------------   --------------   --------------   --------------

Salience (n): the quality of being particularly noticeable or important; prominence. [a]

Synonyms [t]: *wart, blob, bunch*
Antonyms [t]: *depression, ingrowth, lack*

Word Use
Diana's salience made her very desirable to all of the doctor's in the dentistry field.

Pictures
Salience = sailing
Definition = everyone wanted to go on the boat

Story = The fisherman had the largest sail boat and everyone wanted to go sailing with him.

Section 9 Quiz

1. Decimate ___
2. Endurance ___
3. Instill ___
4. Nocturnal ___
5. Salience ___

a. Kill, destroy, or remove a large percentage or part of.
b. Of, relating to, or occurring in the night.
c. The quality of being particularly noticeable or important; prominence.
d. The ability or strength to continue or last, especially despite fatigue, stress, or other adverse conditions; stamina.
e. To introduce by gradual, persistent efforts; implant.

UNIT 4

SECTION 10

Abnormal (adj): deviating from what is normal or usual, typically in a way that is undesirable or worrying. [g]

Synonyms [t]: *bizarre, extraordinary, irregular*
Antonyms [t]: *common, ordinary, usual*

Word Use [g]
The illness is recognizable from the patient's abnormal behavior

Pictures
abnormal = abs + gnome
Definition = strange knot

Story = The gnome with a 6-pack abs, tied together a weird and strange looking knot.

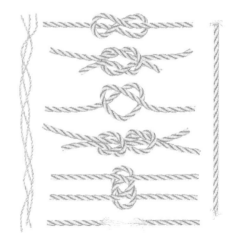

Geniality (adj): Having a pleasant or friendly disposition or manner. [a]

***Synonyms** [t]: amenity, jollity, joy*
***Antonyms** [t]: gloom, woe, coolness*

Word Use [d]
A genial disposition; a genial host.

Pictures
Geniality = Genie
Definition = Smile

Story = When the genie popped out of the bottle, it had a very big smile on its face.

--------------- --------------- --------------- --------------- ---------------

Insurrectionists (n): The act or an instance of open revolt against civil authority or a constituted government. [a]

***Synonyms** [t]: agitator, heretic, revolter*
***Antonyms** [t]: adherent, ally, loyalist*

Word Use [d]
Of course, without American logistical aid, the insurrection would have ended in tragedy.

Pictures
Insurrectionists = Insert + Rock
Definition = Throwing at white house

Story = The anarchist inserted rocks into a launcher and tossed them towards the white house.

Malign (v): To make evil, harmful, and often untrue statements about (someone). [a]

***Synonyms** [t]: bad, evil, malefic*
***Antonyms** [t]: aiding, benign, nice*

Word Use [d]
The gloomy house had a malign influence upon her usually good mood.

Pictures
Malign = Mama +lied
Definition = untrue statement

Story =The mama lied to her child by telling him that dogs don't go to heaven; an untrue statement.

--------------- --------------- --------------- --------------- ---------------

Pedantic (adj): Characterized by a narrow, often ostentatious concern for academic knowledge and formal rules [a]

***Synonyms** [t]: stilted, arid, dry*
***Antonyms** [t]: plain, simple, informal*

Word Use [d]
The problem was that Sorkin did too much (pedantic, predictable) telling and not enough showing.

Pictures
Pedantic = Mouse pad + attic
Definition = getting larger by consuming knowledge.

Story = The mouse pad was consuming all of the detailed knowledge from the computer. It began to expand from all the knowledge the computer was transmitting that it could no longer fit in the attic.

Section 10 Quiz

1. Abnormal ___
2. Geniality ___
3. Insurrectionists ___
4. Malign ___
5. Pedantic ___

a. The act or an instance of open revolt against civil authority or a constituted government.
b. deviating from what is normal
c. To make evil, harmful, and often untrue statements about (someone).
d. Having a pleasant or friendly disposition or manner.
e. Characterized by a narrow, often ostentatious concern for academic knowledge and formal rules

SECTION 11

Opulence (n): Great abundance or extravagance. [a]

Synonyms [t]: excess, goods, riches
Antonyms [t]: dearth, lack, poverty

Word Use [d]
The scale, opulence and fantasy so prevalent a few miles away on the Strip is nowhere to be found.

Pictures
Opulence = operation + ambulance
Definition = abundance of blood

Story = The EMTs had to quickly operate the patient in the ambulance because he was losing a great abundance of blood.

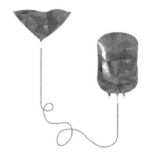

Phonemes (n): any of the abstract units of the phonetic system of a language that correspond to a set of similar speech sounds (such as the velar \k\ of cool and the palatal \k\ of keel) which are perceived to be a single distinctive sound in the language [m]

Synonyms [t]: *characters, rune, signs*
Antonyms [t]: *n/a*

Word Use [d]
The vocabulary is different but the syntax and phonemes are nearly identical.

Pictures
Phonemes = Pho + Knee
Definition = can't differentiate between sounds

Story = The vast majority of the population can't differentiate between Vietnamese pho and Thailand pho because they both taste the same, sound the same when slurping the noodles, and both get eaten while sitting on your knees.

--------------   --------------   --------------   --------------   --------------

Sedulous (adj): Persevering and constant in effort or application; assiduous. [a]

Synonyms [t]: *active, busy, tireless*
Antonyms [t]: *n/a*

Word Use [d]
Sedulous flattery.

Pictures
Sedulous = seed + lace
Definition = climb the hill

Story = the seeds were using a shoelace to climb up the hill because they wanted to get to the top.

Taciturn (adj): Characterized by reserve or a lack of expression. [a]

Synonyms [t]: *aloof, dour, dumb*
Antonyms [t]: *communicative, fluent, wordy*

Word Use [d]
No one would confuse him the taciturn, forgetful and vengeful Senate Majority Leader.

Pictures
Taciturn = Taxi + Turn
Definition = lack

Story =The taxi's GPS was lacking a battery and it made the driver turn into a wrong street.

--------------- --------------- --------------- --------------- ---------------

Viable (adj): Capable of success or continuing effectiveness; practicable. [a]

Synonyms [t]: *applicable, feasible, usable*
Antonyms [t]: *impossible, unlikely, unpractical*

Word Use [d]
A period of history that few teachers can make viable for students.

Pictures
Viable = Violin + Knuckles
Definition = successful and applicable

Story = After many years of persistent practice, Jenn became the most successful and applicable violin musician in her school. Her knuckles show proof of her hard work and dedication.

Section 11 Quiz

1. Opulence ___
2. Phonemes ___
3. Sedulous ___
4. Taciturn ___
5. Viable ___

a. Characterized by reserve or a lack of expression.
b. The smallest phonetic unit in a language that is capable of conveying a distinction in meaning, as the m of mat and the b of bat in English.
c. Persevering and constant in effort or application; assiduous.
d. Great abundance or extravagance.
e. Capable of success or continuing effectiveness; practicable.

SECTION 12

Beret (n): A round, soft, brimless cap that fits snugly and is often worn angled to one side. [a]

Synonyms [t]: *beanie, fez, tam*
Antonyms [t]: *n/a*

Word Use [d]
I went out and bought a beret and a paperback entitled How to Direct le Film.

Pictures
Beret = Bear + Ferret
Definition = Round Beret hat

Story = The bear and the ferret had matching round beret hats.

Dalliance (n): Casual romantic or sexual activity. [a]

***Synonyms** [t]:* delay, poking, toying
***Antonyms** [t]:* push, hurrying, rush

Word Use [d]
Despite plenty of gossip in Copenhagen cafes, no politician has ever been booted from office because of a dalliance.

Pictures
Dalliance = dandelion dancing
Definition = making out

Story = The couple picked up some dandelions that were dancing and started kissing at the park.

--------------- --------------- --------------- --------------- ---------------

Fastidious (adj): Showing or acting with careful attention to detail. [a]

***Synonyms** [t]:* choosy, nice, picky
***Antonyms** [t]:* unfussy, uncareful, uncouth

Word Use [d]
A fastidious eater.

Pictures
Fastidious = Fast Toad
Definition = jumping on lily pads

Story = The fast toad was jumping around quickly, carefully, and accurately on the lily pads.

Infest (v): To live as a parasite in or on. [a]

Synonyms [t]: *abound, annoy, fill*
Antonyms [t]: *n/a*

Word Use [d]
Sharks infested the coastline.

Pictures
Infest = In Festival
Definition = Fleas

Story = The fleas were having a festival on the cat's back.

--------------   --------------   --------------   --------------   --------------

Knead (v): To squeeze, press, or roll with the hands, as in massaging. [a]

Synonyms [t]: *massage, rub, aerate*
Antonyms [t]: *destroy, idle, pull*

Word Use [d]
She kneaded her fist into her palm.

Pictures
Knead = Knee
Definition = massage hands

Story = I went to the massage parlor and the lady used her knees to massage my hands.

Section 12 Quiz

1. Beret ___
2. Dalliance ___
3. Fastidious ___
4. Infest ___
5. Knead ___

a. Showing or acting with careful attention to detail.
b. Casual romantic or sexual activity.
c. To squeeze, press, or roll with the hands, as in massaging.
d. To live as a parasite in or on.
e. A round, soft, brimless cap that fits snugly and is often worn angled to one side.

SECTION 13

Mordant (adj): Bitingly sarcastic. [a]

Synonyms *[t]: acerbic, biting, acerb*
Antonyms *[t]: calm, kind, mild*

Word Use [d]
I like that the emotional lives of women are tinged with a kind of mordant humor for the most part.

Pictures
Mordant = More + Ant
Definition = sarcastic

Story = The more the ants drank coffee the more hyper they got and began to be sarcastic with the jokes they were making.

Orthodox (adj): Adhering to the accepted or traditional and established faith, especially in religion. [a]

Synonyms [t]: *canonical, legitimate, right*
Antonyms [t]: *heterodox, unconventional, unorthodox*

Word Use [d]
Orthodox Jews have voted Republican in every presidential election since 2004.

Pictures
Orthodox = Ortho (braces dentist) Doctor
Definition = Star of David

Story = The Orthodontist Doctor wore the Star of David around his neck to represent his Orthodox Jewish religion values while placing braces.

--------------- --------------- --------------- --------------- ---------------

Principle (n): A basic truth, law, or assumption. [a]

Synonyms [t]: *basis, truth, usage*
Antonyms [t]: *ambiguity, effect, end*

Word Use [d]
A person of good moral principles.

Pictures
Principle = Prince + Simple
Definition = truth and law (Bible + Gavel)

Story = The prince's advisors told him to always keep two simple rules, always say the truth and keep the law, while showing him a Bible and a gavel.

Raiment (n): Clothing; garments. [a]

Synonyms [t]: *apparel, array, clothes*
Antonyms [t]:

Word Use [d]
When she turned to Elsa I saw her eye run in a rapid anxious glance over her daughter's raiment.

Pictures
Raiment = Rain + men
Definition = clothing

Story = The unexpected rain had the working men change clothing into rain coats.

--------------   --------------   --------------   --------------   --------------

Serene (adj): Unaffected by disturbance; calm or peaceful. [a]

Synonyms [t]: *cool, quite, content*
Antonyms [t]: *agitated, loud, noisy*

Word Use [d]
A serene landscape; serene old age.

Pictures
Serene = siren
Definition = meditating

Story = As the siren was going off, the monk kept meditating

Section 13 Quiz

1. Mordant ___
2. Orthodox ___
3. Principle ___
4. Raiment ___
5. Serene ___

a. Bitingly sarcastic.
b. Adhering to the accepted or traditional and established faith, especially in religion.
c. Unaffected by disturbance; calm or peaceful.
d. Clothing; garments.
e. A basic truth, law, or assumption.

UNIT 5

SECTION 14

Aloof (adv): Emotionally reserved or indifferent. [a]

***Synonyms** [t]: detached, haughty, standoffish*
***Antonyms** [t]: compassionate, kind, warm*

Word Use [d]
They always stood aloof from their classmates.

Pictures
aloof = Loaf of bread
Definition − "by itself"

Story = The loaf of bread was by itself and emotionally detached before the main course arrived.

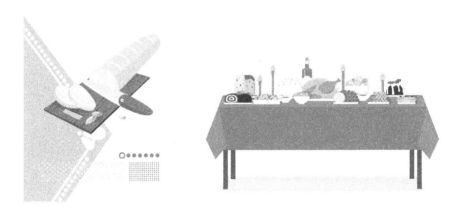

Cohesive (n): Tending to cohere or stick together [c]

Synonyms [t]: *united, adhesive, connected*
Antonyms [t]: *divided, friable, crumbling*

Word Use [d]
A cohesive agent.

Pictures
Cohesive = Coworker and Adhesive
Definition = sticking together

Story = The two coworkers used adhesive tape to stick the balloons together.

---------------   ---------------   ---------------   ---------------   ---------------

Deference (n): respect and esteem due a superior or an elder. [a]

Synonyms [t]: *yielding, capitulation, complaisance*
Antonyms [t]: *fight, disobedience, impoliteness*

Word Use [g]
He addressed her with the deference due to age

Pictures
Deference = "Da" + Fence
Definition = respect

Story = Da child did not cross the fence because he respected the older gentleman's property.

Landmark (n): A prominent identifying feature of a landscape. [a]

Synonyms [t]: marker, tree, hill
Antonyms [t]: whole

Word Use [d]
The post office served as a landmark for locating the street to turn down.

Pictures
Landmark = Land + Marker
Definition = Eiffel Tower

Story = On the land was the Eiffel Tower and a young girl wrote all over it with a pink marker.

---------------   ---------------   ---------------   ---------------   ---------------

Nuisance (n): One that is inconvenient, annoying, or vexatious; a bother. [a]

Synonyms [t]: blister, drag, louse
Antonyms [t]: aid, cheer, joy

Word Use [d]
A monthly meeting that was more nuisance than pleasure.

Pictures
Nuisance = new sauce
Definition = bitter tasting hot sauce / not enjoyable

Story = The new hot sauce was very annoying and didn't make the hot wings enjoyable to eat.

Section 14 Quiz

1. Aloof ___
2. Cohesive ___
3. Deference ___
4. Landmark ___
5. Nuisance ___

a. Tending to cohere or stick together
b. One that is inconvenient, annoying, or vexatious; a bother.
c. Respect and esteem due a superior or an elder.
d. A prominent identifying feature of a landscape.
e. Emotionally reserved or indifferent.

SECTION 15

Exhilarating (adj): making one feel very happy, animated, or elated; thrilling. [a]

Synonyms [t]: exciting, thrilling, tonic
Antonyms [t]: boring, depressing, worrying

Word Use [d]
The cold weather exhilarated the walkers.

Pictures
Exhilarating = Exhale + Hilarious
Definition = making one feel very happy

Story = The comedian warned everyone that the show was going to make everyone very happy. He gave instructions on how to breathe and exhale if the show got too hilarious.

Incompetent (adj): Lacking qualities necessary for effective conduct or action. [a]

***Synonyms** [t]: inept, raw, unfit*
***Antonyms** [t]: able, capable, adept*

Word Use [d]
His incompetent acting ruined the play.

Pictures
Incompetent = in computer + tent
Definition = recycled for not working properly

Story = Inside the computer was an old hardware, it didn't work properly and it had to be thrown in the tent.

--------------- --------------- --------------- --------------- ---------------

Maxim (n): a short, pithy statement expressing a general truth or rule of conduct. [g]
***Synonyms** [t]: adage, belief, canon*
***Antonyms** [t]: n/a*

Word Use [d]
the maxim that actions speak louder than words

Pictures
Maxim = Maxim magazine
Definition = one word

Story = There was just one word in the entire Maxim magazine, and it spoke volumes for how great the magazine was.

Philistine (n): A member of a people, perhaps of Aegean origin, who settled ancient Philistia around the 12th century bc. [a]

Synonyms [t]: barbarian, crude, raw
Antonyms [t]: chaste, clean, gay

Word Use [d]
I'm a philistine, and not ashamed; so was Molière—so was Cervantes.

Pictures
Philistine = Philly + Sting
Definition = Ancient (12th century)

Story = The philly- steak restaurant was so old people started to call it the
"ancient 12th century sting bing."

--------------   --------------   --------------   --------------   --------------

Redress (n): Satisfaction for wrong or injury; reparation. [a]

Synonyms [t]: amends, atonement, indemnity
Antonyms [t]: penalty, sympathy, damage

Word Use [d]
the power to redress the grievances of our citizens

Pictures
Redress = Red Dress
Definition = gift for being innocent

Story = The girl was given a red dress as a reparation for wrongfully being accused for a crime that she didn't commit.

Section 15 Quiz

1. Exhilarating ___
2. Incompetent ___
3. Maxim ___
4. Philistine ___
5. Redress ___

a. Lacking qualities necessary for effective conduct or action.
b. making one feel very happy, animated, or elated; thrilling.
c. Satisfaction for wrong or injury; reparation.
d. A member of a people, perhaps of Aegean origin, who settled ancient Philistia around the 12th century bc.
e. A short, pithy statement expressing a general truth or rule of conduct.

SECTION 16

Correlation (n): A relationship or connection between two things based on co-occurrence or pattern of change. [a]

Synonyms [t]: parallel, match, pendant
Antonyms [t]: difference, disconnection. Imbalance

Word Use [d]
Studies find a positive correlation between severity of illness and nutritional status of the patients.

Pictures
Correlation = apple core + lesion
Definition = Being slit on each side

Story = In order for the apple core to come out symmetrical, the lesions were done in a precise and accurate manner.

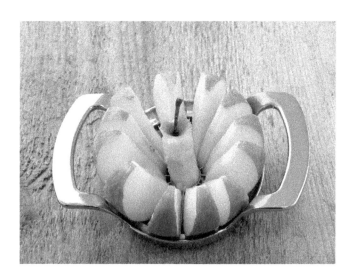

Elusion (n): The act or an instance of eluding or escaping; evasion. [a]

Synonyms *[t]: evasion, dodging, recoil*
Antonyms *[t]: advance, coming, stay*

Word Use [d]
The act or an instance of eluding or escaping; evasion

Pictures
Elusion = A Luge
Definition = evading the competition.

Story = The Olympian was racing down the track on the luge and was evading the challenger.

--------------- --------------- --------------- --------------- ---------------

Idiosyncrasy (n): A structural or behavioral characteristic peculiar to an individual or group. [a]

Synonyms *[t]: eccentricity, trait, bit*
Antonyms *[t]: normality, usualness*

Word Use [d]
The English idiosyncrasy is in that awful external slovenliness too, causing it, and being caused by it.

Pictures
Idiosyncrasy = Idol (Simon Cowell) singing
Definition = Picking Nose

Story = American Idol judge, Simon Cowell, had this peculiar characteristic of picking his nose before singing.

Ought (v): Used to indicate obligation or duty. [a]

Synonyms [t]: *concern, need, tax*
Antonyms [t]: *benefit, distrust, freeing*

Word Use [d]
He ought to be punished. You ought to be ashamed.

Pictures
Ought = Otter
Definition = paying taxes

Story = The otter paid its taxes to the IRS after building his dam because he was obligated to do so.

--------------- --------------- --------------- --------------- ---------------

Solace (n): Comfort in sorrow, misfortune, or distress; consolation. [a]

Synonyms [t]: *condolence, pity, relief*
Antonyms [t]: *discord, disharmony*

Word Use [d]
The minister's visit was the dying man's only solace.

Pictures
Solace = sol (sun)
Definition = show support

Story = El sol went near the moon to show its support while the moon was mourning the loss of the astronauts.

Section 16 Quiz

1. Correlation ___
2. Elusion ___
3. Idiosyncrasy ___
4. Ought ___
5. Solace ___

a. Comfort in sorrow, misfortune, or distress; consolation.
b. Used to indicate obligation or duty.
c. A structural or behavioral characteristic peculiar to an individual or group.
d. A relationship or connection between two things based on co-occurrence or pattern of change.
e. The act or an instance of eluding or escaping; evasion.

SECTION 17

Assuage (v): To make (something burdensome or painful) less intense or severe. [a]

Synonyms *[t]: allay, sate, calm*
Antonyms *[t]: incite, upset, anger*

Word Use [d]
To assuage one's grief; to assuage one's pain.

Pictures
Assuage = a sausage
Definition = unhook a clamp

Story = The sausage was in pain as it was being held by a clamp, until the bun came and unhooked it.

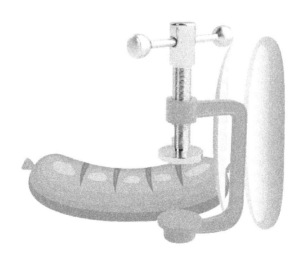

Devious (n): Departing from the correct or accepted way; erring. [a]

***Synonyms** [t]: deceitful, fraudulent, underhanded*
***Antonyms** [t]: forthright, frank, artless*

Word Use [d]
A devious course.

Pictures
Devious = Devilish costume
Definition = robbing a bank

Story = The man wearing a devilish costume robbed the bank and ran away from the police.

--------------- --------------- --------------- --------------- ---------------

Furbish (v): To brighten by cleaning or rubbing; polish. [a]

***Synonyms** [t]: buff, rub, gloss*
***Antonyms** [t]: damage, dull, ruin*

Word Use [d]
To furbish a run-down neighborhood; to furbish up one's command of a foreign language.

Pictures
Furbish = Furby
Definition = to polish

Story = The Furby doll was polishing his brand new luxurious car.

Judicious (adj): Having or exhibiting sound judgment; prudent. [a]

Synonyms [t]: astute, sane, keen
Antonyms [t]: careless, rash, foolish

Word Use [d]
Judicious use of one's money.

Pictures
Judicious = Judge
Definition = listening closely and judging the case

Story = The judge listened to the witness testimony and made a sound judgement to let the case go.

--------------   --------------   --------------   --------------   --------------

Paraphernalia (n): The articles used in a particular activity; equipment. [a]

Synonyms [t]: gear, regalia, effects
Antonyms [t]: n/a

Word Use [d]
A skier's paraphernalia.

Pictures
Paraphernalia = Parrot + Fern
Definition = coat

Story = The parrot wore a fern coat to the bird gathering.

Unit 5

Section 17 Quiz

1. Assuage ___
2. Devious ___
3. Furbish ___
4. Judicious ___
5. Paraphernalia ___

a. Having or exhibiting sound judgment; prudent.
b. To make (something burdensome or painful) less intense or severe.
c. To brighten by cleaning or rubbing; polish.
d. The articles used in a particular activity; equipment.
e. Departing from the correct or accepted way

SECTION 18

Grating (n): sounding harsh and unpleasant. [a]

Synonyms [t]: *dry, shrill, harsh*
Antonyms [t]: *nice, pleasing, smooth*

Word Use [d]
His constant chatter grates on my nerves.

Pictures
Grating = Grater (cheese)
Definition = harsh and unpleasant sound

Story = The customer complained of the harsh and unpleasant sound that the cheese grater made.

Latent (adj): Present or potential but not evident or active. [a]

Synonyms [t]: *lurking, contained, inferred*
Antonyms [t]: *active, live, open*

Word Use [d]
A latent emotion.

Pictures
Latent = Laying down + Tent
Definition = The giant was on top of

Story = The giant man was lying on top of the tent so the animals wouldn't see him.

--------------- --------------- --------------- --------------- ---------------

Obfuscate (v): To make so confused or opaque as to be difficult to perceive or understand. [a]

Synonyms [t]: *baffle, cloud, fog*
Antonyms [t]: *clarify, explain, reveal*

Word Use [d]
To obfuscate a problem with extraneous information.

Pictures
Obfuscate = Elf + Skate
Definition = difficult tricks

Story = The elf was doing very difficult tricks on his skateboard that made the giraffe twisted its neck out of confusion.

Quibble (n): A trivial matter or minor concern raised in arguing or finding fault. [a]

***Synonyms** [t]: nicety, cavil, shift*
***Antonyms** [t]: facing, niggle, shift*

Word Use [d]
He can quibble that he favored "a managed bankruptcy"— without the use of federal funds.

Pictures
Quibble = Queen + Dribble
Definition = arguing about double dribbling

Story = The queen was dribbling a basketball and argued with the ref that she didn't double dribble.

--------------- --------------- --------------- --------------- ---------------

Solicitous (adj): characterized by or showing interest or concern. [a]

***Synonyms** [t]: affection, altruism, grace*
***Antonyms** [t]: animosity, hatred, cruelty*

Word Use [d]
Solicitous about a person's health.

Pictures
Solicitous = Solicitor + Sole
Definition = showing interest

Story = The solicitor was going around the neighborhood showing interest to buy shoes with broken sole.

Section 18 Quiz

1. Grating ___
2. Latent ___
3. Obfuscate ___
4. Quibble ___
5. Solicitous ___

a. To make so confused or opaque as to be difficult to perceive or understand.
b. characterized by or showing interest or concern.
c. sounding harsh and unpleasant.
d. A trivial matter or minor concern raised in arguing or finding fault.
e. Present or potential but not evident or active.

UNIT 6

SECTION 19

Anecdote (n): A short account of an interesting or humorous incident. [a]

Synonyms [t]: *episode, tale, yarn*
Antonyms [t]: *n/a*

Word Use [d]
This anecdote is about as close as Custer gets to being likeable.

Pictures
Anecdote = Neck + Dot
Definition = "Funny/interesting"

Story = Nick had an interesting story of how he's neck got a pink dot.

Unit 6

Delinquency (n): Failure to do what law or duty requires. [a]

Synonyms [t]: *default, crime, fault*
Antonyms [t]: *accomplishment, achievement, success*

Word Use [d]
Delinquency in payment of dues.

Pictures
Delinquency = Deli + currency
Definition = failure to follow the law

Story = The manager at the deli shop had a shortage of currency and failed to follow the law by not paying his employees.

--------------- --------------- --------------- --------------- ---------------

Extant (adj): Still in existence; not destroyed, lost, or extinct. [a]

Synonyms [t]: *actual, current, real*
Antonyms [t]: *dead, extinct, gone*

Word Use [d]
There are only three extant copies of the document.

Pictures
Extant = Exam + Ant
Definition =Alive

Story = The exam taken by many ants, passed and it kept them alive.

Lattice (n): An open framework made of strips of metal, wood, or similar material overlapped or overlaid in a regular, usually crisscross pattern. [a]

Synonyms [t]: frame, grating, net
Antonyms [t]: solid

Word Use [d]
They say the ladder construct is out, lattice is in, for men and women.

Pictures
Lattice = Latte + ice
Definition = wooden framework

Story = The vanilla latte with lots of ice was accidently spilled over the beautiful wooden framework.

--------------   --------------   --------------   --------------   --------------

Pillage (v): To rob of goods by force, especially in time of war; plunder. [a]

Synonyms [t]: desecrate, gut, lift
Antonyms [t]: give, receive, help

Word Use [d]
The barbarians pillaged every conquered city.

Pictures
Pillage = Pill + Village
Definition = Robber

Story = The robber went to the village to steal all of the pills and medication for his dying mother.

Section 19 Quiz

1. Anecdote ___
2. Delinquency ___
3. Extant ___
4. Lattice ___
5. Pillage ___

a. Still in existence; not destroyed, lost, or extinct.
b. To rob of goods by force, especially in time of war; plunder.
c. An open framework made of strips of metal, wood, or similar material overlapped or overlaid in a regular, usually crisscross pattern.
d. Failure to do what law or duty requires.
e. A short account of an interesting or humorous incident.

SECTION 20

Fawning (v): To exhibit affection or attempt to please, as a dog does by wagging its tail, whining, or cringing. [a]

Synonyms [t]: *bowing, abject, humble*
Antonyms [t]: *aloof, cool, proud*

Word Use [d]
The courtiers fawned over the king.

Pictures
Fawning = Fawn (deer) + yawn
Definition = affection

Story = The baby fawn cuddle next to his mother showing affection to his sleepy, yawning mother.

Inconspicuous (adj): Not readily noticeable. [a]

***Synonyms** [t]: dim, faint, shy*
***Antonyms** [t]: open, unhidden, exposed*

Word Use [d]
On Costa Rica Street, in Palermo Soho, there is an inconspicuous black gate.

Pictures
Inconspicuous = Intercom + spit
Definition = notice

Story = As the man kept speaking in the intercom, his spit was piling up but no one could notice it.

--------------   --------------   --------------   --------------   --------------

Nominal (adj): Of, resembling, relating to, or consisting of a name or names. [a]

***Synonyms** [t]: puppet, simple, stated*
***Antonyms** [t]: actual, important, real*

Word Use [d]
A nominal treaty; the nominal head of the country.

Pictures
Nominal = gnome + owl
Definition = Hi my name is badge

Story = The gnome and the owl wore their "Hi my name" is badges at the meeting.

Vocabulary Words Brilliance

Resurgence (n): A continuing after interruption; a renewal. [a]

Synonyms [t]: *comeback, rebirth, rebound*
Antonyms [t]: *failure*

Word Use [d]
Part of the reason for his resurgence, however, is his considerable political skills.

Pictures
Resurgence = Red surge protector + dance
Definition = tripped and continued dancing

Story = While dancing the man tripped over the red surge protector, he immediately got up and continued dancing with his wife.

--------------- --------------- --------------- --------------- ---------------

Wily (adj): skilled at gaining an advantage, especially deceitfully. [g]

Synonyms [t]: *cagey, arch, foxy*
Antonyms [t]: *frank, honest, open*

Word Use [d]
They were wily, changing their car tags along the road and possibly tossing their cell phones.

Pictures
Wily = Wii+ Lily flower
Definition = cheat and be cunning

Story = Everyone knows not to play the Wii with the Lilly flower girl because she tends to cheat and be cunning.

Section 20 Quiz

1. Inconspicuous ___
2. Fawning ___
3. Nominal ___
4. Resurgence ___
5. Wily ___

a. Of, resembling, relating to, or consisting of a name or names.
b. skilled at gaining an advantage, especially deceitfully.
c. Not readily noticeable.
d. To exhibit affection or attempt to please, as a dog does by wagging its tail, whining, or cringing.
e. A continuing after interruption; a renewal.

SECTION 21

Banal (adj): so lacking in originality as to be obvious and boring. [g]

Synonyms [t]: *bland, trite, vapid*
Antonyms [t]: *new, sharp, fresh*

Word Use [d]
A banal and sophomoric treatment of courage on the frontier.

Pictures
Banal = Bone + Owl
Definition = Simple and ordinary

Story = The bone looked too simple and ordinary, so the owl threw it away.

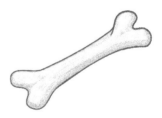

Quintet (n): A composition for five voices or five instruments. [a]

***Synonyms** [t]: band, cast, trio*
***Antonyms** [t]: fraction, individual, part*

Word Use [d]
But even if they fail at that, beating this quintet would make for a huge silver lining.

Pictures
Quintet = Queen + King Tut
Definition = playing 5 different instruments

Story = The queen and king tut were 5 different instruments, the violin, flute, trumpet, piano, guitar, and saxophone, in an orchestra.

--------------   --------------   --------------   --------------   --------------

Stationary (adj): Not capable of being moved; fixed. [a]

***Synonyms** [t]: immobile, static, inert*
***Antonyms** [t]: active, moving, unfixed*

Word Use [d]
The market price has remained stationary for a week.

Pictures
Stationary = police station
Definition = staying in one place

Story = at the police station, they held all of the criminals in one place and told them not to move.

Vocabulary Words Brilliance

Tribulations (n): An experience that tests one's endurance, patience, or faith. [a]

Synonyms [t]: grief, woe, worry
Antonyms [t]: delight, peace, relief

Word Use [d]
But there are those who believe that humans have a role to play in the tribulation.

Pictures
Tribulations = Tribe + Late
Definition = harsh weather and endure.

Story = The indigenous tribe had to face the harsh weather and endure the wait for the late buffaloes to be captured for food.

--------------   --------------   --------------   --------------   --------------

Vacillate (v): To be unable to choose between different courses of action or opinions; waver. [a]

Synonyms [t]: dither, waffle, reel
Antonyms [t]: remain, stay, hold

Word Use [d]
His tendency to vacillate makes him a poor leader.

Pictures
Vacillate = Bass + Late
Definition = having a hard time deciding

Story = My brother was having a hard time deciding whether to buy the red or brown bass that we were late for dinner.

Section 21 Quiz

1. Banal ___
2. Stationary ___
3. Tribulations ___
4. Quintet ___
5. Vacillate ___

a. So lacking in originality as to be obvious and boring.
b. An experience that tests one's endurance, patience, or faith.
c. A composition for five voices or five instruments.
d. To be unable to choose between different courses of action or opinions; waver.
e. Not capable of being moved; fixed.

SECTION 22

Myriad (adj): Constituting a very large, indefinite number; innumerable. [a]

Synonyms [t]: gobs, variable, untold
Antonyms [t]: bounded, calculable, limited

Word Use [d]
The myriad stars of a summer night.

Pictures
Myriad = Mirror Ad
Definition = Price at infinite

Story = The mirror in the weekly ad was featured at an infinite price.

Placebo (n): A substance that has positive effects as a result of a patient's perception that it is beneficial rather than as a result of a causative ingredient. [a]

Synonyms [t]: inactive drug, inactive medicine, sugar pill
Antonyms [t]: n/a

Word Use [d]
The second is the placebo effect, which will often cause anything presented as medication to "work."

Pictures
Placebo = Plastic Elbow
Definition = real looking part

Story = The plastic elbow felt and looked extremely real to the A.I robotics director that he couldn't tell whether if it was fake or not.

--------------- --------------- --------------- --------------- ---------------

Succinct (adj): Characterized by clear, precise expression in few words; concise and terse. [a]

Synonyms [t]: blunt, pithy, terse
Antonyms [t]: lengthy, long-winded, polite

Word Use [d]
The scenes are succinct, by and large; the pattern of the characters rolls right along, whether you catch their drift or not.

Pictures
Succinct = Sexy
Definition = few short words

Story = The groom whispered a few short sexy words into the bride's ear.

Translucent (adj): (of a substance) allowing light, but not detailed images, to pass through; semitransparent. [a]

Synonyms [t]: *luminous, glassy, lucent*
Antonyms [t]: *blocked, cloudy, opaque*

Word Use [d]
Frosted window glass is translucent but not transparent.

Pictures
Translucent = train-tracks loose
Definition = couldn't see through the colored glassed tracks

Story = The colored glassed train tracks were not allowing us to see through it to witness the awesome looking diamonds underneath it

--------------- --------------- --------------- --------------- ---------------

Urban (adj): Characteristic of the city or city life. [a]

Synonyms [t]: *civic, civil, central*
Antonyms [t]: *country, rural, suburban*

Word Use [d]
He is an urban type.

Pictures
Urban = Herb + Van
Definition = The city

Story = All the herbs were outside the city, so we packed our van in quest to finding the natural herbs.

Section 22 Quiz

1. Myriad ___
2. Placebo ___
3. Succinct ___
4. Translucent ___
5. Urban ___

a. Characteristic of the city or city life.
b. Characterized by clear, precise expression in few words; concise and terse.
c. of a substance) allowing light, but not detailed images, to pass through; semitransparent.
d. Constituting a very large, indefinite number; innumerable.
e. A substance that has positive effects as a result of a patient's perception that it is beneficial rather than as a result of a causative ingredient.

SECTION 23

Apathy (n): Lack of interest or concern, especially regarding matters of general importance or appeal; indifference. [a]

***Synonyms** [t]: episode, tale, yarn*
***Antonyms** [t]: n/a*

Word Use [d]
The system is geared towards rewarding intense participation and punishing self-marginalization and apathy.

Pictures
Apathy = Ape + path
Definition = "Lack of interest"

Story = The ape lacked interest to walk the same path as the other apes.

Unit 6

Deliberate (adj): carefully weighed or considered; studied; intentional [a]

Synonyms [t]: *conference, consideration, consultation*
Antonyms [t]: *carelessness, disregard, ignorance*

Word Use [d]
Moving away from the city and all its advantages required a deliberate decision.

Pictures
Deliberate = Dill Pickle + Beretta Gun
Definition = scale

Story = The dill pickle thought hard about shooting his Beretta gun at the weight scale.

--------------   --------------   --------------   --------------   --------------

Harbored (n): A place of shelter; a refuge. [a]

Synonyms [t]: *board, guard, screen*
Antonyms [t]: *forget, harm, open*

Word Use [d]
The old inn was a harbor for tired travelers.

Pictures
Harbored = Hard + bored
Definition = Shelter

Story = The baker was having a hard time finding shelter because he was tired and bored of looking.

Ostracism (n): The act of banishing or excluding. [a]

Synonyms *[t]: avoidance, exile, isolation*
Antonyms *[t]: acceptance, allowance*

Word Use [d]
Shame and ostracism are not guaranteed to be effective; like the recalcitrant husband, Israel may indeed dig in.

Pictures
Ostracism = ostrich + racing
Definition = Banish

Story = The new law has banished the act of ostriches racing during hot days, so instead they were excluded and saw the bunnies race on the track instead.

---------------   ---------------   ---------------   ---------------   ---------------

Sphericity (n): The sky, appearing as a hemisphere to an observer. [a]

Synonyms *[t]: circularity, oneness, wholeness*
Antonyms *[t]: n/a*

Word Use [d]
The sphericity of the globe was thus made matter of certainty.

Pictures
Sphericity = Sphere + City
Definition = saw the sphere

Story = As soon as the skydiver jumped out of the plane he saw the sphere curvature of the city.

Section 23 Quiz

1. Apathy ___
2. Deliberate ___
3. Harbored ___
4. Ostracism ___
5. Sphericity ___

a. The act of banishing or excluding.
b. A place of shelter; a refuge.
c. Lack of interest or concern, especially regarding matters of general importance or appeal; indifference.
d. The sky, appearing as a hemisphere to an observer.
e. carefully weighed or considered; studied; intentional

UNIT 7

SECTION 24

Cryptic (adj): Of Secret or occult. [a]

Synonyms *[t]: arcane, mystic, unclear*
Antonyms *[t]: clear, sure, seen*

Word Use [d]
A cryptic message.

Pictures
Cryptic = Cry + tick
Definition = mysterious

Story = The puppy was crying loudly because the tick was mysteriously hiding behind the ear.

Innate (adj): Existing naturally or by heredity rather than being learned through experience. [a]

***Synonyms** [t]: inborn, connate, natural*
***Antonyms** [t]: n/a*

Word Use [d]
An innate defect in the hypothesis.

Pictures
Innate = gnat (bug)
Definition = flying naturally

Story = The gnats were able to naturally fly the instant they were born.

--------------- --------------- --------------- --------------- ---------------

Nettle (n): Any of various hairy, stinging, or prickly plants. [a]

***Synonyms** [t]: annoy, chafe, fret*
***Antonyms** [t]: aid, assist, calm*

Word Use [d]
She was a nettle in which the rustle of the cassock was visible.

Pictures
Nettle = Needle
Definition = Cactus prickly

Story = The cactus was full of prickly needles.

Reconcile (v): To reestablish a close relationship between. [a]

Synonyms [t]: *appease, conform, harmonize*
Antonyms [t]: *agitate, incite, fight*

Word Use [d]
Matt Latimer on why the GOP needs to reconcile itself to a Romney-Perry fight.

Pictures
Reconcile = Raccoon + ceiling
Definition = forgiving owner

Story = The raccoon came down from the ceiling after his owner forgave him for ripping his shoes.

--------------- --------------- --------------- --------------- ---------------

Subversion (n): the undermining of the power and authority of an established system or institution. [a]

Synonyms [t]: *sabotage, disruption, overthrow*
Antonyms [t]: *n/a*

Word Use [d]
But first, Chicago delegates discussed pressing issues of the day, from Communist subversion to the ongoing Korean War.

Pictures
Subversion = submarine + vision (periscope)
Definition = run away from police

Story = The submarine went submerged under water to escape the police boat, while looking to see if the coast was clear with its periscope.

Section 24 Quiz

1. Cryptic ___
2. Innate ___
3. Nettle ___
4. Reconcile ___
5. Subversion ___

a. To reestablish a close relationship between.
b. Of Secret or occult.
c. the undermining of the power and authority of an established system or institution.
d. Any of various hairy, stinging, or prickly plants.
e. Existing naturally or by heredity rather than being learned through experience.

SECTION 25

Belie (v): To give a false representation to; misrepresent. [a]

Synonyms *[t]: negate, deny, oppose*
Antonyms *[t]: approve, aid, help*

Word Use [d]
His trembling hands belied his calm voice.

Pictures
Belie = Bee + lying
Definition = "False representation; misrepresent"

Story = The bee was lying down pretending to be dead as the dog sniffed it.

Unit 7

Consecrated (v): To declare or set apart as sacred. [a]

Synonyms [t]: hallowed, sanctified
Antonyms [t]: n/a

Word Use [d]
To consecrate a new church building.

Pictures
Consecrated = Concert + Crate
Definition = Set apart

Story = The concert was so loud the baby was put in a crate off to the side with a pacifier.

--------------- --------------- --------------- --------------- ---------------

Keepsake (n): Something that one keeps because of the memories it calls to mind. [a]

Synonyms [t]: memento, relic, favor
Antonyms [t]: n/a

Word Use [d]
But Dick slapped the pocketbook to which he had transferred his keepsake from Miss Ravenden.

Pictures
Keepsake = Key +Snake
Definition = memories

Story = The child lost the key to his picture box where he kept all the memories of his past snake pet.

Utmost (adj): Being or situated at the most distant limit or point; farthest. [a]

Synonyms [t]: olute, full, last
Antonyms [t]: beginning, part, starting

Word Use [d]
He did his utmost to finish on time.

Pictures
Utmost = Up + moist
Definition = farthest

Story = The cross-country boys had to run up to the highest mountain and pass the forest which was moist and wet. Whoever ran the farthest distance would win the title of "fastest runner."

--------------- --------------- --------------- --------------- ---------------

Vehement (adj): Characterized by forcefulness of expression or intensity of emotion or conviction; fervid. [a]

Synonyms [t]: angry, furious, hot
Antonyms [t]: calm, cool, meek

Word Use [d]
Her year in the life sounds dizzying, but there is nothing dizzy about her vehement refusal to name names.

Pictures
Vehement = Via-payment
Definition = Angry and forcefully

Story = The customer at the nail salon forgot to bring her cash at the time of service, the worker angry and forcefully asked her to make a via-payment through her phone.

Section 25 Quiz

1. Belie ___
2. Consecrated ___
3. Keepsake ___
4. Utmost ___
5. Vehement ___

a. Something that one keeps because of the memories it calls to mind.
b. To give a false representation to; misrepresent.
c. To declare or set apart as sacred.
d. Characterized by forcefulness of expression or intensity of emotion or conviction; fervid.
e. Being or situated at the most distant limit or point; farthest.

SECTION 26

Disarming (adj): Tending to allay suspicion or hostility; winning favor or confidence: a disarming smile. [a]

***Synonyms** [t]: irresistible, ingratiating, convincing*
***Antonyms** [t]: despicable, disgusting*

Word Use [d]
A disarming smile.

Pictures
Disarming = Dislocating + arm
Definition = to charm (kisses)

Story = During a wrestling match one of the wrestlers dislocated another wrestler's arm to charm the ladies who were watching, while blowing kisses to them.

Insipid (adj): Lacking flavor or zest; not tasty. [a]

Synonyms [t]: banal, trite, mild
Antonyms [t]: original, tasty, exciting

Word Use [d]
An insipid personality.

Pictures
Insipid = sippy cup
Definition = baby spitting out juice

Story = The baby drank from the sippy cup and quickly tossed it to the floor after spitting out the sour juice.

--------------- --------------- --------------- --------------- ---------------

Prospectus (n): A formal summary of a proposed venture or project. [a]

Synonyms [t]: catalog, list, plan
Antonyms [t]: n/a
Word Use [d]
Don't buy the new stock offering until you read the prospectus carefully.

Pictures
Prospectus =Protractor + Speck
Definition = catalog

Story = The student had a catalog of school supplies he needed to buy before school started it included a ruler, protractor and a speck of articulating paper.

Soporific (adj): Inducing or tending to induce sleep. [a]

Synonyms [t]: *calming, dozy, dull*
Antonyms [t]: *upsetting, awake, exciting*

Word Use [d]
He sounds like a soporific senator defending the ugly compromises of Washington.

Pictures
Soporific = saw + pear
Definition = falling asleep on the job

Story = The lumberjack man was sawing a piece of wood while eating an apple and he fell asleep on the job

--------------- --------------- --------------- --------------- ---------------

Vacate (v): To cease to occupy (a lodging or place); leave. [a]

Synonyms [t]: *abandon, depart, quit*
Antonyms [t]: *allow, come, do*

Word Use [d]
We will have to vacate when our lease expires.

Pictures
Vacate = Bye + Kate Winslet (Titanic)
Definition = abandon

Story = Jack abandoned and said bye to Kate Winslet on the ocean as the Titanic was sinking.

Section 26 Quiz

1. Disarming ___
2. Insipid ___
3. Prospectus ___
4. Soporific ___
5. Vacate ___

a. Tending to allay suspicion or hostility; winning favor or confidence: a disarming smile.
b. Inducing or tending to induce sleep.
c. A formal summary of a proposed venture or project.
d. To cease to occupy (a lodging or place); leave.
e. Lacking flavor or zest; not tasty.

SECTION 27

Flotsam (n): Goods floating on the surface of a body of water after a shipwreck or after being cast overboard to lighten the ship. [a]

Synonyms [t]: *cargo, jetsam, junk*
Antonyms [t]: *n/a*

Word Use [d]
The flotsam of the city slums in medieval Europe.

Pictures
Flotsam = Float (Root-beer float)
Definition = floating ice cream

Story =The ice cream was floating on top of the root beer.

Overhaul (v): To examine or go over carefully for needed repairs. [a]

Synonyms [t]: *fix, rebuild, doctor*
Antonyms [t]: *break, hurt, ruin*

Word Use [d]
My car was overhauled by an expert mechanic.

Pictures
Overhaul = Oven + hot
Definition = needed to be repaired

Story = The baker was having a hard time baking his cakes because his oven was not hot enough, he later found out his oven needed to be repaired so he called an oven repairman.

---------------   ---------------   ---------------   ---------------   ---------------

Secluded (adj): Removed or remote from others; solitary. [a]

Synonyms [t]: *lonely, retired, alone*
Antonyms [t]: *open, populated, friendly*

Word Use [d]
A secluded cottage.

Pictures
Secluded = Sick + Igloo
Definition = remove

Story = The villagers had to remove all the sick and weak patients to an igloo that was closer to the Doctors campground.

Truism (n): A statement that is obviously true or that is often presented as true. [a]

Synonyms [t]: adage, axiom, saying
Antonyms [t]: n/a

Word Use [d]
It is a truism that tough times make people seek out mindless escapes.

Pictures
Truism = Threw
Definition = when he was saying

Story = Nobody believed little John when he was saying he threw the ball 600 ft., even though it was absolutely true.

--------------- --------------- --------------- --------------- ---------------

Wry (adj): Funny in an understated, sarcastic, or ironic way. [a]

Synonyms [t]: droll, awry, dry
Antonyms [t]: straight, straightforward

Word Use [d]
A wry grin.

Pictures
Wry = Cry
Definition = Full of sarcasm

Story = After a long first day of work, Annie went home crying because her new coworkers were very sarcastic and she could not understand them.

Section 27 Quiz

1. Flotsam ___
2. Overhaul ___
3. Secluded ___
4. Truism ___
5. Wry ___

a. To examine or go over carefully for needed repairs.
b. Goods floating on the surface of a body of water after a shipwreck or after being cast overboard to lighten the ship.
c. A statement that is obviously true or that is often presented as true.
d. Removed or remote from others; solitary.
e. Funny in an understated, sarcastic, or ironic way.

SECTION 28

Beset (v): To attack from all sides. [a]

Synonyms [t]: invade, attack, bug
Antonyms [t]: clarify, aid, lose

Word Use [d]
To be beset by enemies; beset by difficulties.

Pictures
Beset = Bed Set
Definition = being attacked by pillows

Story = While he was on top of the bed set, his brothers attacked him with pillows.

Efficient (adj): achieving maximum productivity with minimum wasted effort or expense. [g]

Synonyms [t]: ability, skill, talent
Antonyms [t]: idleness, lack, disability

Word Use [d]
It is a small agency; there are no efficiency gains to be realized by making it another bureau within Commerce.

Pictures
Efficient = Fishing
Definition = lightly tugged on fishing pole to get a fish

Story = The fisherman was fishing and gently pulled on his pole to catch the 80 pound fish.

---------------   ---------------   ---------------   ---------------   ---------------

Quiescence (adj): Quiet, still, or inactive. [a]

Synonyms [t]: calm, quiet, rest
Antonyms [t]: action

Word Use [d]
Rapture was self-transcending, which led to quiescence, tranquility, and catharsis.

Pictures
Quiescence = Choir + Incense
Definition = singing quietly

Story = The choir was lip synching quietly when the smell of the incense filled the room.

Vacuous (adj): Lacking intelligence; stupid or empty-headed. [a]

Synonyms [t]: blank, dull, inane
Antonyms [t]: aware, full, intelligent

Word Use [d]
A vacuous way of life.

Pictures
Vacuous = Vacuum
Definition = had no idea/blank

Story = The sales representative, Patrick Star, was selling a vacuum but had no idea how it worked when the potential buyer asked questions he would blank out.

--------------- --------------- --------------- --------------- ---------------

Zenith (n): The point on the celestial sphere that is directly above the observer. [a]

Synonyms [t]: acme, roof, topper
Antonyms [t]: base, bottom, nadir

Word Use [d]
As summer reaches its zenith, these landscapes provide a welcome touchstone to seasons past.

Pictures
Zenith = See + Venus
Definition = highest point

Story = In order to see the Planet Venus, Venus Williams needed to be at the highest point of the hill, 20 minutes before sunrise or after sunset.

Section 28 Quiz

1. Beset ___
2. Efficient ___
3. Quiescence ___
4. Vacuous ___
5. Zenith ___

a. The point on the celestial sphere that is directly above the observer.
b. Achieving maximum productivity with minimum wasted effort or expense.
c. To attack from all sides.
d. Quiet, still, or inactive.
e. Lacking intelligence; stupid or empty-headed.

UNIT 8

SECTION 29

Bemoan (v): To express grief over; lament. [a]

Synonyms [t]: deplore, rue, milk
Antonyms [t]: be happy, praise, gloat

Word Use [d]
To bemoan one's fate.

Pictures
Bemoan = Bee + moon
Definition = crying

Story = The bee was crying on the moon because his friends stayed on Earth.

Dishabille (n): The state of being partially or very casually dressed. [a]

Synonyms [t]: nakedness, nudity, starkness
Antonyms [t]: clothed

Word Use [d]
She looked at him as though she had noticed his dishabille for the first time.

Pictures
Dishabille = Dishes + Bill (dollar)
Definition = Carelessly dressed

Story = After washing the dishes, Dollar Bill was covered in water stains. He decided not to change and went carelessly dressed to the Christmas party.

--------------- --------------- --------------- --------------- ---------------

Legitimate (adj): Being in compliance with the law; lawful. [a]

Synonyms [t]: fair, lawful, just
Antonyms [t]: abnormal, invalid, unreal

Word Use [d]
The property's legitimate owner.

Pictures
Legitimate = Ledge + mat
Definition = American Flag on property

Story = The store owner placed an American flag on the ledge which had a mat to show that he was the owner and was in compliance with the law.

Resumption (n): The act or an instance of resuming; a beginning again. [a]

Synonyms [t]: *continuation, reopening, restoration*
Antonyms [t]: *n/a*

Word Use [d]
Elements of the pro-Israel lobby have also been on Capitol Hill lobbying for a resumption of U.S. aid to Egypt.

Pictures
Resumption = Resume
Definition = new beginning

Story = The college student was updating his resume because he was looking for a new job and wanted to start a new beginning.

--------------- --------------- --------------- --------------- ---------------

Unique (adj): Characteristic only of a particular category or entity. [a]

Synonyms [t]: *different, lone, single*
Antonyms [t]: *common, like, trite*

Word Use [d]
Bach was unique in his handling of counterpoint.

Pictures
Unique = Unicycle
Definition = different and peculiar

Story = The neighbor's unicycle was designed in a very different and peculiar way, instead of having one wheel it had 3 on top of each other.

Unit 7

Section 29 Quiz

1. Bemoan ___
2. Dishabille ___
3. Legitimate ___
4. Resumption ___
5. Unique ___

a. The state of being partially or very casually dressed.
b. Characteristic only of a particular category or entity.
c. The act or an instance of resuming; a beginning again.
d. Being in compliance with the law; lawful.
e. To express grief over; lament.

SECTION 30

Conducive (adj): Tending to cause or bring something about. [a]

Synonyms [t]: helpful, produce, leading
Antonyms [t]: useless, adverse, hindering

Word Use [d]
Good eating habits are conducive to good health.

Pictures
Conducive = conducting electricity
Definition = bring about lightning

Story = The scientist was using a high voltage conductive electrical battery and it brought about a lot of lightning.

Foraging (n): Plant material that livestock graze or that is cut and fed to them. [a]

Synonyms [t]: *comb, scour, beat*
Antonyms [t]: *aid, give, help*

Word Use [d]
A foraging people.

Pictures
Foraging = Forest + Aging (old)
Definition = koala eating

Story = The koala in the forest was eating all of the old aging leaves.

--------------- --------------- --------------- --------------- ---------------

Pseudonym (n): A fictitious name, especially a pen name. [a]

Synonyms [t]: *alias, handle, aka*
Antonyms [t]: *actual name*

Word Use [d]
And he could not have been seeking fame, for he used a pseudonym.

Pictures
Pseudonym = sewing domino
Definition = sewing a false name with a pen

Story = The old lady was using a pen to sew a false name on the domino

Tactile (adj): Relating to, involving, or perceptible to the sense of touch. [a]

***Synonyms** [t]: palpable, tactual, solid*
***Antonyms** [t]: n/a*

Word Use [d]
These tactile projects make them "feel they can start and finish something," she said.

Pictures
Tactile = Tic Tac on tile
Definition = bumpy feeling

Story = The Tic Tac glued on the tile made it feel very bumpy

--------------- --------------- --------------- --------------- ---------------

Wizen (v): To dry up; wither or shrivel. [a]

***Synonyms** [t]: drain, dry, parch*
***Antonyms** [t]: dampen, fill, grow*

Word Use [d]
And, if he mentioned who he was, could not the wizen man by his side help him to get at them?

Pictures
Wizen = Wizard
Definition = shrivel and dry up

Story = The wizard cast his magic spell on the ant and it made it shrivel and dry up.

Section 30 Quiz

1. Conducive ___
2. Foraging ___
3. Pseudonym ___
4. Tactile ___
5. Wizen ___

a. Plant material that livestock graze or that is cut and fed to them.
b. Tending to cause or bring something about.
c. To dry up; wither or shrivel.
d. Relating to, involving, or perceptible to the sense of touch.
e. A fictitious name, especially a pen name.

SECTION 31

Discrepancy (n): Divergence or disagreement, as between facts or claims; difference. [a]

Synonyms [t]: *difference, distinction, miscalculation*
Antonyms [t]: *accord, agreement, alikeness*

Word Use [d]
The discrepancy between the evidence and his account of what happened led to his arrest.

Pictures
Discrepancy = Disc + crepe
Definition = Disagree

Story = One individual wanted to use a disc as a plate to eat his crepe while the other individual wanted to use a regular paper plate.

Impudent (adj): Offensively bold or disrespectful; insolent or impertinent. [a]

Synonyms *[t]: brazen, cool, flip*
Antonyms *[t]: humble, modest, polite*

Word Use [d]
The student was kept late for impudent behavior.

Pictures
Impudent = In + putty
Definition = disrespectful

Story = The student in the classroom was being disrespectful and kept throwing putty slime at the girls. They got very upset with him.

--------------   --------------   --------------   --------------   --------------

Mentor (n): A wise and trusted counselor or teacher. [a]

Synonyms *[t]: adviser, coach, trainer*
Antonyms *[t]: pupil, student*

Word Use [d]
She spent years mentoring to junior employees.

Pictures
Mentor = Men + tear
Definition = trusted wise man

Story = The men at the pub began tearing up and crying when their drinks weren't ready because they trusted the wise old man outside the pub who told them they provided speedy service here.

Spurned (v): To reject with disdain or contempt. [a]

Synonyms [t]: *despise, disdain, reject*
Antonyms [t]: *accept, allow, love*

Word Use [d]
Yet as the spurned god fades away, Captain Kirk feels a pang.

Pictures
Spurned = Sparrow burned
Definition = didn't want help

Story = The sparrow that was burning rejected the help of the fireman because of his red outfit.

--------------- --------------- --------------- --------------- ---------------

Zeitgeist (n): The spirit of the time; the taste and outlook characteristic of a period or generation. [a]

Synonyms [t]: *climate, feeling, milieu*
Antonyms [t]: *old-fashioned*

Word Use [d]
Which just goes to show that if you wait long enough to reboot, the Zeitgeist will eventually catch up with you.

Pictures

Zeitgeist = Sight (binoculars) + Guy
Definition = generation

Story = John was able to sight see with his binoculars the old house where his grandpa and his guy friends stayed when they went to college after almost two generations. It brought back so many great memories.

Section 31 Quiz

1. Discrepancy ___
2. Impudent ___
3. Mentor ___
4. Spurned ___
5. Zeitgeist ___

a. Offensively bold or disrespectful; insolent or impertinent.
b. The spirit of the time; the taste and outlook characteristic of a period or generation.
c. A wise and trusted counselor or teacher.
d. Divergence or disagreement, as between facts or claims; difference.
e. To reject with disdain or contempt.

SECTION 32

Congeal (v): To solidify or coagulate. [a]

Synonyms *[t]: curdle, dry, jell*
Antonyms *[t]: heat, melt, thin*

Word Use [d]
The fat congealed on the top of the soup.

Pictures
Congeal = Cone + gel
Definition = cooling and rising

Story = The cone full of liquid gel was placed in the freezer and the gel rose to the top as it became cool.

Devious (n): Departing from the correct or accepted way; erring. [a]

Synonyms [t]: *deceitful, fraudulent, underhanded*
Antonyms [t]: *forthright, frank, artless*

<u>**Word Use**</u> [d]
A devious course.

<u>**Pictures**</u>
Devious = devil + vicious
Definition = underhanded tactics to achieve goals

Story = The devil uses vicious underhanded tactics to achieve his goals to corrupt humanity.

--------------- --------------- --------------- --------------- ---------------

Miscreants (n): one who behaves badly, often by breaking rules of conduct or the law. [a]

Synonyms [t]: *criminal, corrupt, perverse*
Antonyms [t]: *moral, good, nice*

<u>**Word Use**</u> [d]
Perhaps, too, like miscreant HAL 9000, the GOP is warming up to sing, "Daisy, Daisy."

<u>**Pictures**</u>
Miscreants = Missing Crayon
Definition = breaking crayons

Story = The kid was missing half of the crayons in his box because he was always breaking them in defiance to his mom.

Supercilious (adj): Feeling or showing haughty disdain. [a]

Synonyms [t]: *bossy, lofty, nervy*
Antonyms [t]: *humble, modest*

Word Use [d]
To point that out, of course, will only strengthen her sense of being persecuted by supercilious elites.

Pictures
Supercilious = Super + Silly
Definition = haughty attitude

Story = The super-intendent dressed as Supergirl was showing some haughty attitude as she was walking through the classrooms. Unknowing she had toilet paper stuck to the sole of her heel, she looked silly and the kids laughed at her.

--------------- --------------- --------------- --------------- ---------------

Wrest (v): To obtain or remove by pulling with twisting movements. [a]

Synonyms [t]: *exact, wring, take*
Antonyms [t]: *give*

Word Use [d]
To wrest a living from the soil.

Pictures
Wrest = Crest Toothpaste
Definition = snatched it away from my hand

Story = When I reached for the Crest Toothpaste, my sister immediately snatched it away from my hand.

Section 32 Quiz

1. Congeal ___
2. Devious ___
3. Miscreants ___
4. Supercilious ___
5. Wrest ___

a. To solidify or coagulate.
b. Departing from the correct or accepted way
c. To obtain or remove by pulling with twisting movements.
d. Feeling or showing haughty disdain.
e. one who behaves badly, often by breaking rules of conduct or the law.

SECTION 33

Deliberation (n): The act or process of deliberating. [a]

***Synonyms** [t]: conference, consideration, consultation*
***Antonyms** [t]: carelessness, disregard, ignorance*

Word Use [d]
Careful consideration before decision.

Pictures
Deliberation = Deliver + nation
Definition = long consideration

Story = After a long and careful consideration the Queen was able to deliver her speech to the nation and promised to deliver free pizza to all.

Petulant (adj): Unreasonably irritable or ill-tempered; peevish. [a]

***Synonyms** [t]:* cranky, fractious, cross
***Antonyms** [t]:* agreeable, nice, pleasant

Word Use [d]
A petulant toss of the head.

Pictures
Petulant = Pet + Late
Definition = Cranky

Story = The old man across the street got cranky when his pet squirrel came an hour late for feeding time, so he tossed the food in the trash.

--------------- --------------- --------------- --------------- ---------------

Surly (adj): bad-tempered and unfriendly. [a]

***Synonyms** [t]:* boorish, cross, sulky
***Antonyms** [t]:* bright, kind, gentle

Word Use [d]
A surly waiter.

Pictures
Surly = surfing leaf
Definition = hitting something because of the bad temper

Story = The surfing leaf hit the flower in the pedals with its surfboard

Transcend (v): To be greater than, as in quality or intensity; surpass. [a]

Synonyms [t]: eclipse, beat, top
Antonyms [t]: fail, lose, surrender

Word Use [d]
His competitiveness made him want to transcend.

Pictures
Transcend = train set
Definition = bigger and better train set

Story = The new train set that Timmy's mother bought him was much bigger and more intense than his previous modeled train set.

--------------   --------------   --------------   --------------   --------------

Vindication (n): Something that provides evidence or support for a claim or argument. [a]

Synonyms [t]: revenge, justification, compurgation
Antonyms [t]: blame, charge, guilt

Word Use [d]
Poverty was a vindication for his thievery.

Pictures
Vindication = Vent + Vacation
Definition = evidence

Story = Two families were in court because the vent at the vacation home was broken and one family had evidence that they were innocent after showing video proof to the judge.

Section 33 Quiz

1. Petulant ___
2. Surly ___
3. Transcend ___
4. Deliberation ___
5. Vindication ___

a. To be greater than, as in quality or intensity; surpass.
b. Something that provides evidence or support for a claim or argument.
c. Unreasonably irritable or ill-tempered; peevish.
d. bad-tempered and unfriendly.
e. The act or process of deliberating.

ANSWERS FOR QUIZES

Answers for Section 1 Quiz

1. b
2. c
3. a
4. d
5. e

Answers for Section 2 Quiz

1. e
2. b
3. c
4. a
5. d

Answers for Section 3 Quiz

1. d
2. c
3. e
4. b
5. a

Answers for Section 4 Quiz

1. a
2. c
3. b
4. e
5. d

Answers for Section 5 Quiz

1. e
2. a
3. c
4. b
5. d

Answers for Section 6 Quiz

1. b
2. e
3. c
4. d
5. a

Answers for Section 7 Quiz

1. c
2. e
3. d
4. a
5. b

Answers for Section 8 Quiz

1. c
2. e
3. d
4. a
5. b

Answers for Section 9 Quiz

1. a
2. d
3. e
4. b
5. c

Answers for Section 10 Quiz

1. b
2. d
3. a
4. c
5. e

Answers

Answers for Section 11 Quiz

1. d
2. b
3. c
4. a
5. e

Answers for Section 12 Quiz

1. e
2. b
3. a
4. d
5. c

Answers for Section 13 Quiz

1. a
2. b
3. e
4. d
5. c

Answers for Section 14 Quiz

1. e
2. a
3. c
4. d
5. b

Answers for Section 15 Quiz

1. b
2. a
3. e
4. d
5. c

Answers for Section 16 Quiz

1. d
2. e
3. c
4. b
5. a

Answers for Section 17 Quiz

1. b
2. e
3. c
4. a
5. d

Answers for Section 18 Quiz

1. c
2. e
3. a
4. d
5. b

Answers for Section 19 Quiz

1. e
2. d
3. a
4. c
5. b

Answers for Section 20 Quiz

1. c
2. d
3. a
4. e
5. b

Answers for Section 21 Quiz

1. a
2. e
3. b
4. c
5. d

Answers for Section 22 Quiz

1. d
2. e
3. b
4. c
5. a

Answers for Section 23 Quiz

1. c
2. e
3. b
4. a
5. d

Answers for Section 24 Quiz

1. b
2. e
3. d
4. a
5. c

Answers for Section 25 Quiz

1. b
2. c
3. a
4. e
5. d

Answers for Section 26 Quiz

1. a
2. e
3. c
4. b
5. d

Answers for Section 27 Quiz

1. b
2. a
3. d
4. c
5. e

Answers for Section 28 Quiz

1. c
2. b
3. d
4. e
5. a

Answers for Section 29 Quiz

1. e
2. c
3. d
4. a
5. b

Answers for Section 30 Quiz

1. b
2. a
3. e
4. d
5. c

Answers

Answers for Section 31 Quiz

1. d
2. a
3. c
4. e
5. b

Answers for Section 32 Quiz

1. a
2. b
3. e
4. d
5. c

Answers for Section 33 Quiz

1. c
2. d
3. a
4. e
5. b

YOUR GIFTS

As a bonus, you can get my latest **Free Better Memory Now Guide and Memory Training Videos** to help you with your ongoing continued memory improvement education!

Download Here:
www.aemind.com/VocabBookGift

HONEST REVIEW REMINDER

I love seeing the transformation that people go through when they learn this system, and I would be extremely grateful if you helped contribute to that transformation.

When you get a chance, if you could take about a minute or two to go to the Vocabulary Words Brilliance Book Page and leave a Review, you will truly be helping to improve the lives of thousands of people who struggle with their memory

CONTACT

Learn more about Luis Angel's "**Better Memory Now**" programs and other Memory Training material for Professionals, Students, Memory Athletes, and Everyone Else, by going to:

www.AEMind.com

SOCIAL

YT: Youtube.com/aemind
FB: Facebook.com/aemind1
IG: ae.mind
Twitter: @aemind

Email: LuisAngel@AEMind.com

CPSIA information can be obtained
at www.ICGtesting.com
Printed in the USA
BVHW040740210420
578012BV00008B/225